C000024149

RAW IS MORE

VIBRANT RECIPES BURSTING WITH GOODNESS

PHOTOGRAPHY : ISSY CROKER
ILLUSTRATIONS : ANITA MANGAN

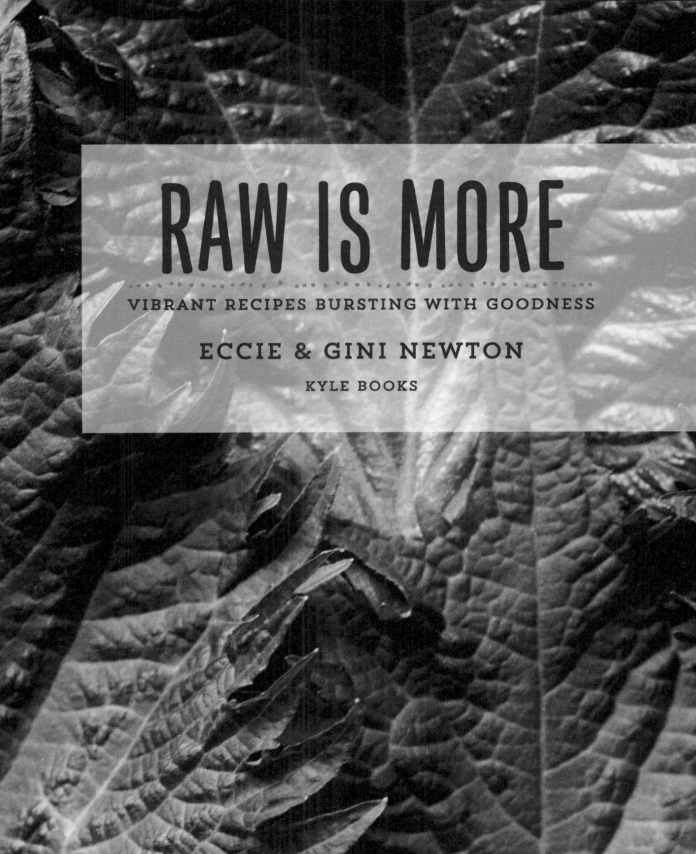

RAW IS MORE

VIBRANT RECIPES BURSTING WITH GOODNESS

ECCIE & GINI NEWTON

KYLE BOOKS

We would like to dedicate this book to our mother who has supported us through everything we have done. Her passion for family and food has made us who we are today.

First published in Great Britain in 2016 by
Kyle Books, an imprint of Kyle Cathie Ltd
192-198 Vauxhall Bridge Road
London SW1V 1DX

general.enquiries@kylebooks.com

www.kylebooks.co.uk

Printer line 10 9 8 7 6 5 4 3 2 1

ISBN 978 0 85783 323 5

Text © 2016 Eccie Newton and Gini Newton
Design © 2015 Kyle Books
Photography © 2015 Issy Croker

Eccie Newton and Gini Newtron are hereby identified as the author of this work in accordance with Section 77 of the Copyright, Designs and Patents Act 1988.

All rights reserved. No reproduction, copy or transmission of this publication may be made without written permission. No paragraph of this publication may be reproduced, copied or transmitted save with written permission or in accordance with the provisions of the Copyright Act 1956 (as amended). Any person who does any unauthorised act in relation to this publication may be liable to criminal prosecution and civil claims for damages.

Designer & Illustrator: Anita Mangan
Photographer: Issy Croker
Food Stylist: Annie Nichols
Props Stylist: Iris Bromet
Editorial Assistant: Hannah Coughlin
Production: Nic Jones, Gemma John and Lisa Pinnell

A Cataloguing in Publication record for this title is available from the British Library.

Colour reproduction by ALTA Image

Printed and bound in China by C&C Offset Printing Co., Ltd.

CONTENTS

'Raw' and 'cookbook' may seem to be contradictory words, so we should say at the start who we are and what 'raw' means to us. We aren't vegans, Gini and I run a company that delivers lunchboxes to the desks of office workers around London each day (karmacans.co.uk), offering both raw and cooked food, and we enjoy a very varied diet of which raw is one part. For us, eating raw food is not a statement, it's a celebration of great ingredients. We've spent the past year exploring recipes and putting quality food first – dairy, grains, vegetables, fruit, sugar, nuts, meat and fish. Raw ingredients are powerful in themselves, packed with beneficial enzymes, vitamins and good bacteria, and using great ingredients makes this kind of cooking simple, tasty and healthy all at the same time.

These days, few of us know where our food comes from, who grew it, what species or breed it is and what it was fed on. We felt that eating raw made us really conscious of the production and seasonality of everything we consumed. When you're not cooking or overly processing anything, which means not roasting or browning, extracting or enhancing flavours through heat, the job you do in preparing these dishes shifts from distilling down flavours to celebrating the unadulterated taste. Some of our favourite recipes in this book are the salads – tomato, beetroot, avocado or fennel – because they require just a few short steps to make, but their impact is huge. When you think just how glorious freshly picked, perfectly ripe fruit and vegetables taste at the peak of their season, why would you want to change that by cooking them?

We want to help you explore food in a whole new way. Take, for example our spicy tacos or pulp cakes (see page 150). Rather than relying on a piece of toast for breakfast, with these two recipes you're packing in fibre, using up old vegetables and bringing great new flavours to kickstart your day. Even better, all our recipes are easy and straightforward, exactly as you would expect from eating raw.

SO WHAT IS RAW FOOD?

The basic idea is that raw means any food that has never been heated above 40°C, and this is essential because higher temperatures will destroy its all-important enzymes. Enzymes perform trillions of vital functions in our bodies and most enzymes operate best at body temperature (37°C), and at a neutral pH7. In essence, without enzymes, we could not digest our food. Enzymes act as catalysts, meaning they enable chemical reactions that allow us – like all living things – to metabolise the food we eat. Without them we would be unable to convert food into energy or to renew the cells that make up our bodies. Unfortunately, many food-manufacturing processes involve high temperatures that render our food effectively 'dead' because the enzymes, vitamins and minerals have been lost.

So, it rapidly becomes clear that the more raw food we introduce into our daily diet, the more we benefit from these live enzymes converting proteins into amino acids – simple molecules that are readily absorbed – and releasing nutrients that give us nourishment and vitality.

Additionally, eating raw is about preserving the good bacteria contained in food and those that are naturally present in our gut – the so-called biotic flora. These bacteria sometimes contain enzymes that

we cannot produce. A great example of this is Lactobacillus acidophilus, a common bacterium used in fermentation processes to make yogurt, soy products and pickles. Lactobacillus contains the enzyme lactase, which helps to break down lactose, which some people cannot digest by themselves. Our gut is made up of a complex array of our own enzymes and other bacteria that digest many molecules that we cannot. The relationship is essential to our survival, we need to 'unlock' these molecules to fuel the chemical reactions inside our body and to replace parts of our bodies that require repair, but we often have to rely on the enzymes made by bacteria to do so.

It's a delicate balance, we need some 'friendly' bacteria, or probiotics, but others will harm us, so eating raw food does not mean you can ignore basic food hygiene in a bid to boost your intake of enzymes and good bacteria. And, if you can, try to buy organic and wash all your fruit and vegetables thoroughly before eating them.

Pickling and preserving is a great way to add flavour to raw dishes and can help aid digestion too.

PROCESSING RAW FOOD

A lot of plant matter requires some 'processing' in order to make it digestible. This is because plants have walls around their cells made from a rigid cellulose that humans cannot digest. The cellulose needs to be broken down for us to be able to access the nutrients it contains. For this reason, eating greens like kale or broccoli raw will serve you little in the way of nutrition unless they are first physically blended or mashed, or cured or pickled in salt, citrus juice or vinegar. Adjusting the temperature or pH

helps your body to process their otherwise inaccessible nutrients.

EATING HEALTHILY

The words 'healthy', 'natural' and 'fresh' get wheeled out a lot in London – literally in the case of our company – and our customers, more than anything, want food that is healthy. For us health is about balance, there is no one way of eating, no magic ingredient or process that can make someone healthy, in fact it's the complete opposite. We strongly feel that the best way to feel great from what you eat is to eat together, to share your food, sitting down at a table with the people you care about, and never to exclude whole food groups from your diet, only to add good things into it, or change the processes used to make it.

We want this book, above all else, to be approachable. When we started this project the one thing we felt that eating raw lacked was the accessibility that made us want to jump right in and start making it for everyone we know. That's fairly ironic because what could be simpler than assembling the most delicious things on a plate for your friends and family? For people who don't have a chance to cook, we really want to tell them that it's okay, you can eat amazing food that's great and you can make dinner for ten people with next to no fuss.

THE BASICS

We've given the option for our recipes to be either oven-dried or dehydrated (where needed) and we've tried to limit the equipment list where possible to a knife, an oven and a food processor or blender.

We don't think you need lots of expensive kit in your kitchen to make something taste delicious – save the cash and spend it on buying great ingredients from people you can really trust and build a good relationship with! That said, dehydrating is a lot of fun, it extends the repetoire of what you can achieve with raw food far beyond simple salads. Dehydration works by circulating air and removing water from the air.

Dehydrators can either look a bit like an oven, or they can be made up of plastic layers with holes in them with the fan underneath, the plastic disc kind can be as little as £30 online, whereas the oven type can cost between £100 and £300. Dehydration in the oven is less effective as a dehydrator and the temperature can be harder to control, that said, it is still possible and definitely worth a go.

One of the main advantages of raw is that timings are much more flexible: nothing's going to burn horribly, and you can't overcook. (For any recipe here that requires 'cooking', you will be setting your oven or dehydrator to the lowest setting possible, ideally to 37°C.) In fact, when it comes to how long to dry things for, often it's just a matter of leaving 'overnight' or until it's pliable rather than an exact number of hours. This means you can get things ready in your own time (many things only take a few minutes) and go and enjoy the party. You get a lot of freedom with raw food and for us, this directly translates into how we eat. Both of us spend long hours in the kitchen each day and when we get home we want simple salads, nothing that takes more than 15 minutes to make, but is refreshing and simple. Equally, on the weekend, there are usually people round and we've found that rather than hovering in the kitchen by the oven we'd rather let people help themselves

to great salads and fresh vegetables, homemade ceviches and gravalax, so we can join in the fun. Serve your friends this way and you'll never be a slave to your stove again.

There are some distinct benefits to eating a diet that includes raw foods – you're cutting out a lot of highly processed foods, where the journey from the raw ingredients to your table, is often long and circumspect. Although there is not yet good or reliable, scientifically-backed evidence to suggest that eating raw enhances your gut flora or benefits the enzyme production, eating raw makes your body work harder for nutrients, fats, proteins and carbohydrates, which means that a raw diet can help keep you in shape. And, with all that fresh ingredients, including plenty of raw food in your diet is cleansing, hydrating and energising. On the flipside, it's important to give your body a helping hand when eating raw long term (by changing the pH of food, crushing, dehydrating or pickling) so your body can extract the nutrients you really need from the food that you eat.

4 REASONS TO GIVE RAW A GO:

(1) Taste more great food.

When you eat raw, you eat produce in its most natural state. Natural, fresh ingredients taste amazing, from crunchy fresh veggies and juicy fruits to super fresh meat and fish.

(2) More real food.

When you choose a raw diet you often choose to make your food from scratch each day. We're careful with what we mean when we say 'processed', because processing food can mean simply chewing it or mashing it. However, often when you buy most of your meals pre-made from a supermarket or from restaurants, many processes go into their production that you probably wouldn't consider good for you. Taking control of those processes and controlling the source of all the ingredients that go into a freshly prepared meal remove some of those extra unnecessary steps from produce to plate.

(3) Eating together.

When you are putting real effort into the food you create, you make time for eating and for the food, so you're less likely to eat in front of the TV and more likely to share with friends and family and celebrate the effort and time that went into your meal.

(4) Health and well-being.

Many people feel more energised, cleansed and hydrated when they include raw food in their diet.

IMPORTANT INGREDIENTS

DAIRY PRODUCE

If you suffer from lactose intolerance you might want to try eating well-aged raw cheeses and yogurts as they contain bacteria that produce the enzyme lactase, which digests lactose into simple sugars that your body can easily absorb. The older the cheese, the more bacteria and the more the lactose has been converted into simple sugars – Parmesan contains next to no lactose at all. Give it a go, as some of this bacteria will remain in your gut and may help to improve lactose digestion.

Milk that is labelled 'organic raw milk' has nothing added or removed. It has not been homogenized or microfiltered, there are no hormones or antibiotics given to the herd – you're looking at a product that's been consumed by people for 7,500 years at least. For us, there's nothing unnatural about that. In the UK, raw milk production is tightly controlled and monitoring herd health of dairy farms is incredibly strict.

Buy your raw milk, cream, yogurt and kefir (a type of yogurt that is packed with enzymes and bacteria) straight from a trusted farm or a single-source dairy. Look for freshness,

which is essential. The colour is normally slightly more yellow than you will be used to – pure white is not natural. Ask whether the cows are organically and grass fed. And buy your raw cheese from a good cheesemonger who can tell you how and where it was made. We like Neal's Yard for British cheeses.

MEAT AND FISH

We've given a lot of space in the book to meat and fish. Obviously they are a great source of good fat and protein, they taste delicious and are among the best food to eat raw. People around the globe have devised incredible methods to prepare the freshest best-quality meat and fish – we've included ceviches and cures, tartares and sushi, made by marinating, pickling, freezing, salting and beating and many of those methods are actually raw.

Get to know your butcher, explain what you are preparing and ask about the different cuts on offer. Try to source beef from cattle that have been grass fed and raised outside and choose meat that has been hung. There is a lot of debate over dry-ageing and hanging meat, but food experts in the UK generally agree that if beef is properly hung microorganisms begin to break down the muscle fibre and some of its water content will drain off, improving both the texture and flavour of the meat – you're looking for meat that has been hung for anything over two weeks. Marbling (fat patterns) and a deep rich red wine colour is what you're after. Once you've got your ingredients together, preparing something like tartare will take just a few minutes of chopping, seasoning and tasting.

Get your fish direct from boats or fishmongers who are supplied from sustainable day boats and from dry-land, sustainable fish farms. Look for red bloody gills, bright shining eyes, lots of slime over shiny scales. Any fish should smell

like the sea – not fishy at all. It can be scary handling whole fish so ask your fishmonger to gut, fillet and de-skin your fish for you if you don't feel comfortable doing it yourself.

Our portion size of meat and fish is much less than you would typically eat cooked. Eating 250g of raw steak would be almost impossible, all you need is 120g max per serving. In any case, we recommend eating meat on special occasions and for family meals because raising

cattle and other grazing animals is bad for the environment. We're not vegetarians, but we try to eat a little, top-quality meat and fish no more than a couple of times a week rather than base our everyday meals on meat.

EGGS

Eggs are a great source of protein, vitamins and minerals. Do buy free-range, from a source you trust, and use them as fresh as possible.

Incidentally, you should never wash an egg as it damages the coating around their shells making them porous to bacteria.

FRUIT AND VEGETABLES

Whenever possible, buy unpackaged fruit and veg – small packs of plastic-wrapped beans, broccoli, carrots or salad leaves have been irradiated (gamma rays are passed through the packet) to kill bacteria. The radiation is not intrinsically harmful to the consumer, but it does kill a lot of the bacteria that eating raw seeks to incorporate into the diet. Try to go to farmers' markets or farm shops and you'll be getting local, seasonal produce, too.

Buying frozen can be a good idea as frozen berries, peas and other veggies have all been picked at their best and frozen immediately so they are super fresh. Use your freezer to do the same – experiment with the kinds of fruit and veg suitable for freezing that you can buy when things are in season (and cheaper) and save them for winter.

SEAWEED

Seaweed is great for you. It's packed with nutrients, low in calories and sugar but incredibly high in minerals. It also has an intense flavour and great texture. Seaweeds are available in Asian stores and online.

Kelp Noodles: these clear noodles made from kelp have a great crunch, but little flavour making them a great alternative to cooked noodles or pasta.

Nori: we often eat these dried seaweed sheets with a smoky flavour as a snack. Use them for sushi or blend them into butter.

Mixed dried seaweed: these are sometimes described as sea vegetables, sea greens or mixed sea vegetable salad. We rehydrate these and add them to poke or have them alone with kaiso salad.

FINALLY

We've kept this book as raw as we possibly can, with just one or two non-raw ingredients that we've used where there was no raw alternative. In the case of the Frankie and Summer Rolls, we've used rice paper sheets that are cooked during their manufacturing process, but they are essential to hold together all the wonderful flavours inside. We've added some puffed rice to the Salmon Chirashi and Poke for texture and authenticity. And we've used oatmeal – oats are steamed in order to stabilise them before being sold, this prevents them moulding. You can mill your own oat flakes with a simple grinder if you'd like to avoid eating them cooked, however we have left this out to allow for a quick and easy breakfast and baking choice. We've used some fermented products, where there has been an initial pasteurization step, but followed by a lengthy fermentation where many essential bacteria are cultivated. In these cases we've chosen to keep these products in the book (along with some vinegars) as we feel that they return to a dynamic active bio-culture like that of raw food as well as adding a great deal of flavour and nutrition that isn't available from a product like salt. An example of this is nama shouyu.

BREAKFASTS

PLAIN JANE BIRCHER MUESLI

SERVES 2

Swiss Bircher muesli is made with oatmeal that is soaked in juice overnight, topped with fresh compote, honey, fruit and seeds. We've added a few variations to freshen it up and have used almond milk. Most oats have been steamed for stabilisation, so you can buy raw groats, and flake them yourself, or sprouted oats, but we usually use jumbo oats or oatmeal and soak overnight.

120g jumbo oats or oatmeal

240ml apple juice

240ml raw almond milk

raw kefir, optional, to serve

squeeze of raw honey, to serve

. . . . . ' . . . . ' . . . . . .

Place the oats in a bowl and add the apple juice and almond milk to cover. Stir the ingredients together. Store in a tightly sealed plastic container overnight. Drain off any excess liquid and it's ready. Top with raw kefir and a squeeze of raw honey and enjoy!

ALMOND BUTTER & RASPBERRY BIRCHER MUESLI

SERVES 2

This is our healthy version of a peanut butter and jelly sandwich! It is quite similar in flavour and the sweet and salty taste works well with the soft oats.

150g fresh raspberries, plus extra berries for topping

2 tablespoons raw honey

5 teaspoons raw almond butter

juice of ½ lemon

1 recipe Plain Jane Bircher Muesli (see left)

150ml raw almond milk

2 mint leaves

4 basil leaves

. . . . ' . . . . ' . . . .

Place the berries in a blender with the honey and blend until smooth, then sieve them into a clean bowl discarding the seeds. Don't wash the blender. Put the almond butter and lemon juice into the blender with the sieved raspberries, blend for a couple of seconds until smooth, adding a tablespoon of water, if necessary.

Divide the Bircher muesli between two bowls and mix with the almond milk gradually so it's quite runny, swirl in the almond butter and raspberry mixture, scatter the mint and basil leaves on top.

ALPINE BIRCHER MUESLI

SERVES 2

Our favourite berries for this recipe are blackberries as you can forage for them yourself, but a frozen pack of fruits of the forest is also a good option.

130g fresh blackberries

2 tablespoons raw honey

1 apple

pinch of sea salt (optional)

20g raw butter, melted at 35°C

2 tablespoons crushed raw hazelnuts

2 tablespoons crushed raw almonds

1 recipe Plain Jane Bircher Muesli
   (see page 16)

400ml raw yogurt or kefir

Place the berries in a blender with the honey and blend until smooth.

We like to sieve the mixture to get rid of the bitter little seeds, but if you don't feel like it, don't worry. (This lasts for up to 4 days in the fridge.)

Grate the apple using a mandoline.

Add a pinch of salt to the melted butter, if it's unsalted.

Divide the Bircher muesli base between two bowls, and then top with butter, yogurt or kefir, nuts and the berry compote.

BANANA & YOGURT BIRCHER SMASH

SERVES 2

We had this as children with full fat greek yogurt, and here we have made it with unpasteurised, raw yogurt. Full fat live yogurt is packed with enzymes and keeps you full for longer. Uniquely, dairy products contain both calcium and vitamin D, the vitamin that the body requires to process calcium.

2 bananas

4 tablespoons raw yogurt

1 recipe Plain Jane Bircher Muesli
   (see page 16)

Smash the bananas as aggressively as you can into the yogurt.

Don't drain the excess liquid from your muesli, just stir it in so the oats are nice and moist and swirl them into the yogurt.

TURKISH-INSPIRED BIRCHER MUESLI

Follow the Plain Jane Bircher Muesli recipe (see page 16), but before serving add 2 crushed cardamom pods, a scraping of vanilla pod seeds, grated zest of an unwaxed lemon and orange, a spoonful of golden sultanas and a couple of mint leaves; maybe even some pomegranate seeds and a few chopped dates.

VANILLA, CINNAMON & ALMOND AVOCADO

SERVES 2

5 WAYS WITH AVOCADO

2 ripe avocados

zest and juice of ½ unwaxed lemon

1 teaspoon cold-pressed extra virgin olive oil

seeds scraped from ¼ vanilla pod

1 teaspoon ground cinnamon

1 teaspoon raw cane sugar

¼ teaspoon pink Himalayan rock salt

2 tablespoons raw chopped almonds

4 slices of Raw Seed Bread (see page 120) or Pulp Cakes (see page 150)

This is quite a different breakfast. You might be surprised by the combination of avocado with cinnamon and vanilla, but these aromatics aren't innately sweet and go well with the richness of the avocados.

Stone and peel the avocados and cut lengthways into thickish slices. Marinate the slices in the lemon and oil.

Mix the vanilla seeds, cinnamon, sugar and salt in a bowl with the chopped almonds.

Lay the avocado onto the seed bread and dust with the nut mixture.

TIP

Here's how to peel an avocado: cut into the fruit lengthways as far as the stone and run the knife right round it; twist and separate. Put the half with the stone in the flat of your hand with the stone facing up. With the knife in your other hand, cut down into the stone, hard enough so the knife gets stuck. Twist the knife and the stone will come loose. Pull it out and remove from the knife. Use the knife to peel off the skin, drawing the knife in towards your hand, thumb pressing down onto the skin.

LIME AVOCADO
ON TACOS

SERVES
2

This is a simple, fresh start to the day. We recommend making the tacos a few days in advance, so that in the morning you can make this in under 5 minutes.

2 ripe avocados

1 lime, halved

2½ teaspoons paprika

¼ teaspoon ground coriander

2 tablespoons cold-pressed
    extra virgin olive oil

2 Spicy Tacos (see page 150)

sea salt and freshly ground
    black pepper

Stone and peel the avocados and chop them into cubes. Squeeze the lime juice over.

Toss in the paprika, coriander, oil, salt and pepper.

Serve slighlty mashed on the spicy tacos.

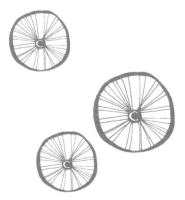

MATCHA AVOCADO

SERVES
2

Matcha, made from the young leaves of a green tea plant, is great for your mind as it is said to keep you awake and focus the brain. Avocados are full of good fat, packed with nutrients and calories, so this is a brilliant way to begin the day.

2 ripe avocados

juice of 1 lemon

1 teaspoon matcha powder

1 teaspoon dried chilli flakes

2 tablespoons cold-pressed
    extra virgin olive oil

2 Pulp Cakes (see page 150)

sea salt and freshly ground
    black pepper

Stone and peel the avocados and chop them into large chunks. Toss with the lemon juice in a bowl.

Dust with matcha powder, chilli flakes, salt and pepper. Drizzle with oil and mash onto the pulp cakes.

AVOCADO WITH HONEY VINAIGRETTE

Our Nana used to make this for us for breakfast. Every time she made it, she used to tell us that she needed to stuff as many avocados as possible into us while we were too small to complain. This was back when the world's best plan for avocados was baking them.

1 ripe avocado

2 tablespoons cold-pressed extra virgin olive oil

1 tablespoon red wine vinegar

1 teaspoon raw honey

a large handful of rocket leaves

sea salt and freshly ground black pepper

Cut the avocado in half, remove the stone, but leave the avocado in its skin.

Mix the oil, vinegar and honey in a small bowl. Pour into the holes left by the stone.

Top with the rocket, roughly chopped or torn over the top, and season.

We recommend mashing it all up with a fork inside the skin and eating it with a spoon.

AVOCADO & QUICK-CURED LEMONS

These sour, cured lemon slices cut through the fattiness of the avocado making this breakfast really refreshing.

2 ripe avocados

6 segments of Quick-cured Lemons (see page 155)

2 tablespoons oil from the jar of Quick-cured Lemons

4 Pulp Cakes (see page 150)

a small handful of coriander leaves

¼ teaspoon crushed coriander seeds

sea salt and freshly ground black pepper

Stone and peel the avocados and cut into chunks. Toss with the cured lemon, lemon oil, salt and pepper.

Divide between the pulp cakes and top with coriander leaves and seeds.

SMALL PLATES

AJO BLANCO

SERVES 4

White gazpacho from Andalucia in Spain is made with almonds and garlic and served with grapes or melon.

300g raw almonds

400ml water

350ml cold-pressed extra virgin olive oil, plus 1 tablespoon oil to serve

½ cucumber

⅛ celery stalk

4 garlic cloves

1 tablespoon sherry vinegar

1 teaspoon salt

½ teaspoon white pepper

10 white grapes, halved

a handful of watercress

First dry out the almonds in the oven at its lowest setting or in a dehydrator at 37°C for 3 hours.

Then, in a high-speed blender, blend together the water, olive oil, cucumber, celery, almonds, garlic and vinegar. Season with salt and white pepper.

Pour into a bowl and chill for an hour in the fridge.

Serve in small bowls, topped with sliced grapes, a drizzle of olive oil and the watercress.

GAZPACHO

SERVES 2

It is important that you like the flavour of the olive oil you choose as it will affect the taste of the soup. It is worth trying a little bit beforehand.

4 tablespoons raw almonds

4 tablespoons water

7 tablespoons cold-pressed extra virgin olive oil

2 tablespoons red wine vinegar or juice of ½ lemon

4 medium very very ripe tomatoes (look for dark red colour on the inside, and really soft flesh)

¾ red pepper

¼ small red onion

1 garlic clove

sea salt and freshly ground black pepper

FOR THE TOPPINGS

½ red pepper, finely chopped

¼ red onion, finely chopped

¼ cucumber, finely chopped

4 tablespoons mixed seeds

In a high-speed blender, blend the almonds until they become a fine meal. Stop the blender.

Add the water, oil and vinegar. Then add the tomatoes, pepper, onion and garlic and start the blender (ensuring the lid is on). Blend for 1 minute, taste, add salt and pepper and blend for a further minute.

Serve in small bowls, scattered with the toppings.

OVEN-DRIED KALE

SERVES 4

Crunchy kale crisps are a yummy alternative to potato crisps. Make a big batch and store in an airtight container for up to a week.

250g kale

½ teaspoon salt

½ teaspoon freshly ground black pepper

1 teaspoon cold-pressed extra virgin olive oil

· ·

Pull the larger, tougher stalks off the kale and tear the leaves into manageable sizes.

In a bowl toss the kale with the salt, pepper and oil.

Put the oven on its lowest setting, or use a dehydrator at 37°C. Spread the kale out on baking parchment on baking trays in one layer with space between the leaves. Dry in the oven overnight or in a dehydrator for 6–7 hours.

OVEN-DRIED KALE WITH TAHINI DRESSSING

SERVES 4

Adding a tahini dressing gives these kale crisps added flavour and umami. These are really moreish!

250g kale

½ teaspoon salt

½ teaspoon freshly ground black pepper

FOR THE TAHINI DRESSING

1 teaspoon cold-pressed extra virgin olive oil

2 tablespoons tahini

1 tablespoon nama shoyu or soy sauce

juice of ½ lemon

1 teaspoon raw honey

· ·

In a small bowl, vigorously beat all the ingredients for the tahini dressing together until smooth and shiny.

In a bowl toss the kale with the salt, pepper and tahini dressing. Put the oven on its lowest setting, or use a dehydrator at 37°C. Spread the kale out on baking parchment paper on baking trays in one layer with space between the leaves and dry for at least 12 hours.

FRANKIE ROLL

SERVES
2

This is a Mumbai street snack, full of flavour and spice, which normally contains fresh veggies inside a roti. Here we've replaced the roti with rice paper wraps, and the traditional filling, which is often made from sliced veggies and mashed potato, is replaced with peas and shredded red cabbage. As with all Mumbai street food, these are fairly spicy, so half the amount of chilli if you like.

6 large rice paper wraps, rinsed in cold water

FOR THE FILLING

100g kelp noodles

200g frozen peas, defrosted in lukewarm water

1 teaspoon ground cumin

1 teaspoon chaat masala

1 teaspoon dried mango powder

½ teaspoon garam masala

1 teaspoon red chilli powder

2 teaspoons raw butter, melted at 35°C

1 teaspoon finely minced ginger

1 teaspoon minced garlic

100g red cabbage, very finely sliced

Use scissors to cut the noodles into manageable lengths. Rinse in cold water for 10 mintes and drain.

Mash the peas up roughly. Toss all the filling spices, butter, ginger and garlic together in a bowl, then add the peas and combine thoroughly. Mix in the noodles and the red cabbage and set aside.

For the onion masala, mix the onion with the masala spices, salt and oil in a separate bowl.

For the chilli pickle, mix the salt, sugar and vinegar in a small bowl until the salt and sugar are dissolved. Then add the chilli and set aside.

FOR THE ONION MASALA

1 red onion, diced into 1cm cubes

1 teaspoon dried mango powder

¼ teaspoon chilli powder

1 teaspoon salt

1 teaspoon cold-pressed rapeseed oil

FOR THE CHILLI PICKLE

½ teaspoon salt

½ teaspoon raw cane sugar

1 tablespoon rice vinegar

1 green chilli, finely chopped

FOR THE CORIANDER CHUTNEY

a large handful of coriander leaves

4 tablespoons water

juice of 1 lime

1 teaspoon minced fresh ginger

2 tablespoons raw kefir or yogurt

pinch of salt

For the coriander chutney, blend all the ingredients until smooth.

Soak the rice paper sheets for about 30 seconds in warmish water so they become supple enough to roll (do this in batches so that you add more to soak while you roll, rather than soaking them all from the beginning and by the time you roll the last one the wrap has been sitting in the water for 25 minutes getting very soggy).

Divide the filling between the wraps – don't overfill them. Add a teaspoon of onion masala to each wrap and a few drops of the chilli pickle. Roll up the wraps, tucking in the ends as you roll and hold your fingers over the filling to keep it in place. Serve the chutney on the side.

COURGETTES WITH CASHEW CREAM & TOMATO SALSA

SERVES 2

1 courgette

FOR THE CASHEW CREAM

1 small packet of raw
  cashews (approx. 50g)

1 garlic clove

1 tablespoon tahini

squeeze of lemon

sea salt and freshly ground
  black pepper

FOR THE SALSA

2 large ripe tomatoes

2 fresh basil leaves, plus
  extra to garnish

1 garlic clove

sea salt and freshly ground
  black pepper

This is perfect for a starter or as a snack. You
could arrange the ingredients in a timbale
mould if you want to impress your guests!

Thinly slice the courgette lengthways with a sharp knife or
mandoline.

To make the cashew cream, blend the cashews in a blender
with the garlic, tahini and a little water until smooth. Add a
sprinkle of salt and pepper and a squeeze of lemon.

To make the salsa, put all the ingredients in a blender for
just 5 seconds – you don't want it to be too smooth.

Arrange the courgette slices in a layer on a serving plate.
Spread the cashew cream over and then add a layer of the
tomato salsa on top. Repeat. Garnish with extra basil leaves.

ROLLING PIN KALE SALAD

400g purple or green kale

zest and juice of 5 unwaxed lemons

FOR THE DRESSING

3 tablespoons tahini

2 tablespoons cold-pressed extra virgin olive oil

2 teaspoons nama shoyu or soy sauce

freshly ground black pepper

The idea of squeezing vegetables to break down the hard cellulose cell wall is nothing new. We've discovered that using a rolling pin makes the task easy. This is perfect for a light summer salad with an amazing crunchy texture that you can't achieve from cooking.

Pull off all the kale stalks and discard. Place the kale leaves on a chopping board and vigorously roll with the rolling pin, pressing down firmly.

Liberally sprinkle the lemon juice over the kale. Continue rolling until the kale starts to soften and become pliable and broken down.

Mix the dressing ingredients together and toss with the kale.

BEETROOT
RAVIOLI

SERVES
2
AS A STARTER

3–4 beetroot

150g soft raw goat's cheese

25g raw almonds, blitzed so
they form almond meal

zest of 1 unwaxed lemon

cold-pressed extra virgin
olive oil

65g frozen petits pois,
defrosted in lukewarm
water

a handful of rocket leaves

5g aged parmesan
(parmigiano reggiano),
finely grated

sea salt and freshly ground
black pepper

This ravioli is so delicious and it is made without flour or eggs
and doesn't need cooking. You will need a mandoline to get
the slices as fine as possible, otherwise they won't shape
around the filling. You're looking for the beetroot to be so thin
you can almost see through it. One problem we had at first
became the dish's saving grace: when we set the mandoline to
its thinnest setting it was very hard to get a whole slice, instead
we kept getting half slices where one side was incredibly thin
and the other side was a little thicker. We laid the thin sides
of two beetroot slices slightly over one another and created a
much larger slightly oblong round with a very thin middle. If
you try to create the two ravioli 'skins' in this way you'll have a
lot more success at creating nice supple round ravioli.

Set the mandoline on its finest setting. Slice the beetroot as
thinly as you can. The slices may be incomplete rounds, with
one end thinner than the other, but that's ok as two thin ends
can be joined to create a larger more flexible circle of beetroot.

In a bowl, combine the goat's cheese, almond meal, the lemon
zest and a few drops of olive oil.

Place one round of beetroot on a board, drop 2 teaspoons of the
goat's cheese mixture into the centre, lay a second round of
beetroot over the goat's cheese ball and press together.

Repeat until you have 6–10 ravioli, then top with the peas,
rocket, parmesan and drizzle with olive oil.

MARINATED AVOCADO WITH PISTACHIOS & SUMAC

SERVES 2

Sumac is the ground berries of the sumac, a tree that grows throughout the Middle East, and it is a common flavour in Turkish dishes. The sourness of the sumac cuts through the avocado, adding zing and texture.

2 ripe avocados

3 teaspoons ground sumac

zest and juice of 1 unwaxed lemon

2 tablespoons cold-pressed extra virgin olive oil

a handful of rocket leaves

3 tablespoons shelled pistachios

4 Pulp Cakes (see page 150)

sea salt and freshly ground black pepper

Stone and peel the avocados and chop into large, evenly sized chunks.

Toss in the sumac, lemon zest and juice, olive oil, salt and pepper.

Roughly chop the rocket and pistachios.

Spoon the avocado mixture onto the pulp cakes and top with the rocket and pistachios.

GUACAMOLE

SERVES 4

The Aztecs invented guacamole, which was originally made using a pestle and mortar. We like to flavour ours with pepper, chilli, spring onion and coriander and serve it with kale chips.

2 very ripe avocados

zest and juice of 2 limes

½ red pepper, deseeded

3 very ripe cherry tomatoes

2 small spring onions

1 long, mild red chilli

5 tablespoons cold-pressed extra virgin olive oil

a small bunch of coriander

sea salt and freshly ground black pepper

Stone, peel and chop the avocados into very small chunks and transfer to a mixing bowl. Pour the lime juice over and toss with a spoon or your hands. Refrigerate the mixture while you prepare the other ingredients.

Chop the pepper very finely. Do the same with the tomato, spring onion and the chilli. Mix the chopped veg into the avocado and roughly mash with a fork.

We like our guacamole quite chunky; some people like it smooth. (If you like it very smooth, we would suggest putting the avocado in a food processor and blending for a few seconds with the lime juice, then transferring to a bowl and adding the chopped veg.)

Mix in the olive oil, salt and pepper. Roughly chop the coriander leaves and finely chop the stalks. Top the guacamole with coriander and lime zest.

HAMACHI & DAIKON WITH PONZU DRESSING

SERVES 2

2 yellowtail amberjack fillets, alternatively use sea bream or any meaty white fish, frozen for 20 minutes to help slicing

1 daikon (Japanese radish)

zest of 1 yuzu or zest of ½ unwaxed lemon and ½ unwaxed orange

FOR THE PONZU DRESSING

120ml nama shoyu or soy sauce

3 tablespoons yuzu juice (using 1 yuzu) or a combination of orange and lemon juice

1 tablespoon water

1 tablespoon mirin (sweet rice wine)

⅛ teaspoon crushed garlic

In Japan, this is made with amberjack, where it is called hamachi. It is a seasonal delicacy in the colder months. You could use fresh yellowtail tuna as an alternative. I (Eccie) ate this dish last year in Japan and what amazed me was the texture of the beautiful ribbons of yellowtail and the radish. Ponzu is essentially soy sauce mixed with yuzu juice. In Japan there's a bit of an obsession with yuzu. It looks just like a satsuma, yet it tastes different – somewhere between a grapefruit, a lemon and a tangerine. If you can't find the fruit, several supermarkets now sell yuzu juice – or try online. A daikon is a long white Japanese radish – if you're struggling to find one, replace it with small round radishes.

Slice the raw fish very thinly with a very sharp knife so that it resembles ribbons.

Thinly slice the daikon into ribbons, using a mandoline or vegetable peeler.

Mix together all the dressing ingredients.

Arrange the fish and daikon on plates, top with yuzu or orange and lemon zest and serve with the ponzu dressing.

SUMMER ROLLS

MAKES
12
ROLLS

24 raw ama-ebi prawns, shells and black intestine removed

2 lemongrass stalks, finely minced

1 butterhead lettuce (you may not want all of it, depending on size)

12 rice paper wrappers

½ packet of kelp noodles, soaked in cold water for 10 minutes then drained well and patted dry

2 carrots, spiralized into noodles

4 spring onions, cut into quarters lengthways

½ cucumber, cut into thin matchsticks

12 coriander stems

12 perilla or shiso leaves

12 thai basil leaves

FOR THE DRESSING

1 garlic clove, crushed

1 thumb-sized piece of peeled ginger, grated

1 small, mild red chilli, minced

3 tablespoons fish sauce

1 star anise

1 tablespoon nama shoyu or soy sauce

3 tablespoons lime

1 tablespoon raw cane sugar

Vietnamese summer rolls are packed full of fresh vegetables giving a crunchy texture with a punchy dipping sauce that brings flavour. We make these using ama-ebi, Greenland shrimp, or deep/cold water shrimp. The name varies, but these shrimp come from around Hokkaido (northern Japan) in the winter, or from the cold Atlantic waters around Greenland and are pink when they are raw. After a couple of days in the fridge these prawns become delicious and sweet (ama-ebi means sweet prawn) and are the only species that are best eaten raw. The overall effect of the filling is quite sweet with the prawn, carrot and the herbs to balance the sour and salty dressing. We've used a spiralizer to make the carrot into noodles here, but you can use a mandoline or a grater to create the same effect. If you can't find perilla or shiso leaves a strong, mustard-flavoured leaf would be fine.

Toss the prawns in the minced lemongrass. Separate out the butter lettuce leaves and rip the large ones in half. Cut the kelp noodles into manageable lengths.

Soak the rice paper sheets for about 30 seconds in warmish water so they become supple enough to roll (do this in batches so that you add more to soak while you roll, rather than soaking them all from the beginning and by the time you roll the last one the wrap has been sitting in the water for 25 minutes getting very soggy).

Place the first sheet onto a clean dry board, add a tiny amount of noodle, carrot, spring onion, cucumber, 1 coriander sprig and a prawn about an eight of the way across the disc of rice paper. Fold the edge over this once. Add the rest of the filling: a perilla leaf, butter lettuce, another prawn, a basil leaf, more noodle and carrot – less is more, the roll shouldn't have too much filling or it will never roll. Then go full burrito, fold the sides into the wrap, and roll up very tightly but without breaking.

Repeat for the other rolls, expect that the final rolls will turn out better than the first one – inevitable really.

Then make the dressing by combining all the ingredients together in a bowl and serving alongside the rolls.

FENNEL & LEMON GRAVALAX

SERVES
2

1kg very fresh salmon fillet, head end, thin edges removed, preferably frozen and thawed, skin on

FOR THE CURE

50g raw cane sugar

70g sea salt (if you're feeling indulgent, you could use 60g Himalayan rock salt and 60g golden caster sugar)

a small bunch of flat-leaf parsley

1 fennel bulb, cut with a mandoline

¼ celery stalk, finely sliced

peel of 3 unwaxed lemons, either zested, or removed with a vegetable peeler

1 teaspoon freshly ground black pepper

FOR THE DIJON & CIDER VINEGAR AIOLI

3 tablespoons Dijon mustard

2 tablespoons cider vinegar

3 tablespoons Aioli (see page 157)

1 tablespoon chopped capers

We really like gravalax, it lasts for ages and when you tell people you made it yourself they'll be really impressed, despite the fact that all you have to do is to put some salt and sugar onto some fish and leave it in the fridge for a few days. We like to freeze the fish before we use it to kill any larger parasites that might be lurking in the salmon. Fennel has such a fresh aniseed flavour. When combined with the oils from the lemon peel, it adds a delicate depth of flavour to the fish.

For a more traditional version, you could use a handful of dill fronds and the peel from 1 lemon instead of the fennel, celery and parsley.

In a large dish, mix all the cure ingredients together.

Place the fish onto the cure skin-side up, sprinkle some of the cure mixture onto the skin, then weight down with a chopping board and leave in the fridge for 48 hours, flipping the fish over every 12 hours.

Remove from the fridge and scrape off the cure thoroughly, it could be an uncomfortable dining experience if you don't – crunchy salty bits everywhere! If you are struggling to remove the salt, you could take a damp unused cloth and wipe it over the fillet.

Thickly slice the salmon and arrange on a plate.

Make the sauce by mixing the mustard and vinegar into the aioli and top with chopped capers.

BEEF CARPACCIO

SERVES
4

600g beef fillet or topside

juice of 3 lemons

1 teaspoon sea salt

FOR THE SALAD

10 ripe cherry tomatoes,
    finely sliced

4 handfuls of rocket leaves

a small handful of flat-leaf
    parsley, very finely chopped

FOR THE ONION MARINADE

juice of 1 lemon

pinch of sea salt

pinch of raw cane sugar

2 tablespoons cold-pressed
    extra virgin olive oil

1 small red onion, sliced as
    finely as possible

FOR THE DRESSING

3 tablespoons cold-pressed
    extra virgin olive oil

3 tablespoons red wine
    vinegar

2 tablespoons raw honey

1 small garlic clove, grated
    or crushed

You can use beef fillet for this; it is the softest cut, making it ideal for eating raw. As it's being sliced so thinly you don't need a lot. As an alternative you can ask your butcher to cut you one long muscle of rump or topside. Use the best meat that you can afford. Aged, free-range and organic beef has a totally different flavour and texture to supermarket beef. Ageing is essential for high-quality meat. In the UK meat can be aged for up to 55 days, by which point enzymes have begun to break down the proteins, resulting in a darker colour, richer flavour and softer texture.

To 'cook' the meat, pour the lemon juice over, dust with salt, wrap in clingfilm and freeze for 3 hours.

While the meat is in the freezer, make the onion marinade. Put the lemon juice in a bowl, add the salt, sugar, onion slices and olive oil. Toss together and set aside.

For the dressing, combine the olive oil and vinegar with the honey and crushed garlic in a bowl and mix together.

Remove the meat from the freezer and slice very thinly using a sharp knife. Divide between four plates and top with a few tomatoes, some of the quick-cured onion slices and a teaspoon of their juice, a handful of the peppery rocket leaves and a teaspoon of chopped parsley. Finish with the dressing drizzled on top.

SALADS

BURMESE TOMATO SALAD

4 ripe tomatoes

a very small bunch of basil

a small bunch of coriander

6–8 small mint leaves

5 tablespoons peanuts, plus
   a few to garnish

¼ teaspoon salt

¼ teaspoon raw cane sugar

1 long red chilli

3 tablespoons dried
   garlic flakes (shop-bought
   or dehydrate very thin
   slices of garlic for 3 hours)

FOR THE DRESSING

2 tablespoons fish sauce

juice of 1½ limes

2 teaspoons raw cane sugar

1 tablespoon groundnut oil

½ small garlic clove

I (Eccie) ate this salad first in Bagan in
Myanmar /Burma and it is a perfect mix of
sour, salty, sweet and spicy.

Cut the tomatoes in half, and then into wedges. Roughly chop
the basil, pick off the coriander leaves from the stalks and cut
the mint leaves in half.

In a small blender, blitz the dressing ingredients and set aside.

Blitz the peanuts with the salt and sugar, chilli and dried garlic
flakes. Pulse the blender and add one-third of the dressing
gradually.

Place the tomatoes on a plate, dress with the remaining
two-thirds of the dressing and top with the peanut, chilli and
garlic mix. Sprinkle with the herbs and remaining few peanuts
and serve.

HEIRLOOM TOMATO SALAD WITH MISO DRESSING

SERVES 6

2kg mixed heirloom tomatoes

½ teaspoon sea salt

200g micro leaves (mizuna, cress, beetroot sprouts, alfalfa sprouts)

a handful of rocket leaves

2 tablespoons dried garlic flakes (shop-bought or dehydrated in very thin slices for 3 hours)

3 tablespoons puffed rice, optional

FOR THE DRESSING

1 tablespoon white miso paste

1 teaspoon red miso paste

1 tablespoon rice wine vinegar

1 tablespoon mirin (sweet rice wine)

2 tablespoons avocado oil

Try to find a mixture of small and large heirloom tomatoes of as many different colours as you can find. We like ripe little yellow ones, giant beefsteaks, green and black tiger ones and long ripe oddly-shaped red ones. When you're cutting them, try to just go along natural cut lines. Really large ones make good slices or wedges and small cherry tomatoes can be halved.

Cut up all the tomatoes into different shapes – wedges, slices, halves and quarters. Toss in the salt and drain in a colander for 20 minutes.

Place the tomatoes on a large flat plate and arrange the micro leaves and rocket over the top.

Mix the dressing ingredients together and spoon over the tomatoes.

Top with the dried garlic and the puffed rice.

BURMESE AVOCADO SALAD

SERVES 4

This is our favourite salad from Myanmar/ Burma.

5 ripe avocados

juice of 1 lime

5 tablespoons peanuts

½ teaspoon salt

1 teaspoon raw cane sugar

3 small firm white onions or shallots, finely sliced

5 curry leaves, torn very finely

a handful of coriander, finely chopped

a handful of basil or thai basil, finely chopped

a handful of mint leaves

4 tablespoons dried onion slices

FOR THE DRESSING

3 tablespoons fish sauce

¼ teaspoon raw cane sugar

1 red chilli, finely chopped

juice of 2 limes

¼ teaspoon nama shoyu or soy sauce

For the dressing, combine all the ingredients and leave in the fridge to infuse while you make the salad.

Stone, peel and chop the avocados into large uniform chunks and toss lightly in a bowl with the lime juice. Do not over-mix as the avocado will become mushy.

Grind the peanuts with the salt and sugar in a pestle and mortar. Toss the onion and herbs with the avocado; add a few spoonfuls of the dressing to taste, toss again, then top with the peanuts and dried onion slices.

TURKISH TOMATO SALAD

SERVES 6

Za'atar is an Eastern Mediterranean spice blend that includes dried thyme and oregano and is popular in a lot of Middle Eastern cooking. It's aromatic, especially when combined with extra virgin olive oil.

2kg cherry tomatoes

sea salt

a small bunch of flat-leaf parsley, roughly chopped

1 tablespoon ground sumac

4 tablespoons pomegranate molasses or the blitzed and sieved juice of 2 pomegranates

zest of 3 unwaxed lemons

2 tablespoons good-quality za'atar

3 tablespoons cold-pressed extra virgin olive oil

freshly ground black pepper

12 Pulp Cakes (see page 150), to serve

Chop the cherry tomatoes into quarters, toss in a pinch of salt, place in a colander and allow to drain over the sink for 20 minutes. If you're making this salad in advance, the draining part is really important – it keeps the tomatoes nice and firm. The salt helps this process along.

Toss the tomatoes in a large bowl with the parsley, sumac, pomegranate molasses, lemon zest, za'atar, olive oil and pepper.

Serve on the pulp cakes.

AVOCADO & GRAPEFRUIT SALAD

A fresh salad with sour grapefruit and rich avocado. Save the membrane of the grapefruit after removing the wedges, to squeeze over the avocado.

2 ripe avocados

2 grapefruit

200g rocket leaves

3 tablespoons cold-pressed extra virgin olive oil

1 chilli, finely chopped

sea salt and freshly ground pepper

Stone and peel the avocados and cut them lengthways into thin slices.

Cut the grapefruit in half horizontally, and then segment, removing all of the translucent membrane with a sharp knife.

Squeeze the juice from the grapefruit membrane into a small bowl. Finely chop the rocket. Arrange the avocado and grapefruit segments on a plate.

Add the oil, salt and pepper and chopped chilli to the grapefruit juice, mix and pour over the salad before serving.

CARROT, RAISIN & CUMIN SALAD

If you make too much of this salad, make flatbreads with the same ingredients. Simply blitz the pine nuts and raisins to a smooth paste, stir in all the other ingredients and then flatten into large rounds on greaseproof paper. Dehydrate on the lowest setting in the oven for 2–3 hours on each side.

4 carrots, peeled and grated or mandolined

2 teaspoons ground cumin

2 teaspoons ground coriander

a small handful of coriander, finely chopped

a small handful of flat-leaf parsley, finely chopped

5 tablespoons cold-pressed extra virgin olive oil

juice of 1 lemon

4 tablespoons raisins

4 tablespoons pine nuts

sea salt and freshly ground black pepper

Toss the grated carrot with the spices, herbs, olive oil and lemon juice and season with salt and pepper.

Top with the raisins and pine nuts.

TURKISH ONION SALAD WITH ZA'ATAR

1 large red onion

zest of 1 unwaxed lemon
and juice of 2 lemons

5 tablespoons cold-pressed
extra virgin olive oil

1 teaspoon sea salt

2 tablespoons Quick-cured
Lemon (see page 155)

2 tablespoons good-quality
za'atar

1 teaspoon ground sumac

1 tablespoon pomegranate
molasses or the blitzed
and sieved juice of 1
pomegranate

Although pomegranate molasses is not
strictly raw, it adds such a great depth of
flavour to this salad, so we decided to use
it, but you can substitute it by blitzing
the seeds from a pomegranate and then
sieving the juice.

Finely slice the onion, place in a bowl and toss with
the lemon juice, olive oil and salt. Leave for at least
10 minutes.

Toss the cured lemon in za'atar, sumac and lemon zest.

Combine the onion and the cured lemon in a serving bowl and
finish with pomegranate molasses.

BABY GEM & ENDIVE SALAD

SERVES 4

Baby gems have a pretty mild flavour, endive leaves are bitter and pungent, but when you add mustard and salt, the bitterness is tempered and becomes another layer of flavour. For a richer aioli, using egg, see page 157.

6 baby gem lettuces
2 endive heads

FOR THE EGG-FREE AIOLI

1 garlic clove
3 heaped tablespoons Dijon mustard
1 teaspoon sea salt
120ml cold-pressed extra virgin olive oil
240ml cold-pressed rapeseed oil
juice of ½ lemon
olives or raw almonds, to serve

First make the aioli. Crush the garlic into a large round glass or heavy ceramic bowl. Add the mustard, salt and start to drip in a little of the two oils.

Whisk in the oil and drip in a bit more, whisk, then allow a constant thin stream of oil to pour into the bowl while you whisk. Add the lemon juice, continue to add oil, and stop when it's thick and yellow.

Quarter the baby gem lettuces lengthways so you have wedges, pick off the endive leaves and tear them in half.

To serve, arrange the lettuces on a plate, spoon on a dollop of aioli and top with olives or almonds.

ONION, PARSLEY & MUSTARD SALAD

SERVES 2

This is a great salad to serve on the side. It's fresh and light and peppery.

FOR THE LEMON-CURED ONION SLICES

1 large red onion
juice of 2 lemons
1 teaspoon sea salt
5 tablespoons cold-pressed extra virgin olive oil
a large handful of flat-leaf parsley
a handful of mustard cress
2 tablespoons black mustard seeds

FOR THE DRESSING

1 teaspoon raw honey
1 tablespoon Dijon mustard
2 tablespoons cold-pressed extra virgin olive oil
squeeze of lemon

Finely slice the onion, place in a bowl and toss with the lemon juice, salt and olive oil. Leave for at least 10 minutes. (It will keep for 2 days in a sealed container in the fridge.)

Roughly chop the parsley and toss with the onion, mustard cress and mustard seeds.

Mix the dressing ingredients together and spoon over as much as is needed to coat the leaves and onion.

FENNEL SALAD

SERVES 2 AS A MAIN   SERVES 4 AS A SIDE

2 fennel bulbs

a small handful of mint
leaves

a small handful of basil
leaves

5 tablespoons cold-pressed
extra virgin olive oil

2 teaspoons raw honey

4 tablespoons cider vinegar

2 garlic cloves, grated or
crushed

1 small chilli, finely chopped

2 fennel bulbs, sliced very
thinly and dehydrated or
Oven-dried Fennel (see
page 153)

1 round or butterhead
lettuce

soft raw cheese

sea salt and freshly ground
black pepper

It's a pretty good day when it's a fennel day. Florence
fennel is the name of the edible bulb, with its
interlocking leaves and delicate stalks and fronds. This
recipe uses a raw cow's milk cheese, called St Jude's
from White Wood Dairy in north Hampshire, but use
any raw soft cheese you like.

Chop the fluffy green fronds off the tops of the fennel and chop
them with the stalks.

Remove one outer leaf of the fennel bulb and cut the bottom
off, then either use a mandoline or finely slice the fennel
lengthways, so you get whole cross sections of beautiful
raw fennel.

If you're eating this immediately, skip this next step. Place the
fennel into a bowl of iced water, cover with a plate and put it in
the fridge until you're ready to serve it. If you don't do this, your
fennel will go brown around the edges as it oxidises.

Chop the herbs very finely; try compressing them into a tight
ball with one hand then slice down with the point of the knife
staying on the board and your hand running down the knife.

In a salad bowl, mix the olive oil, honey, vinegar, grated garlic,
salt and pepper with a fork until fully combined and emulsified,
then add the herbs, chilli, dried and fresh fennel (drain and
dry the fresh fennel first). Tear whole leaves of the lettuce into
the bowl.

Toss in the salad bowl until the dressing has coated all the
leaves and fennel.

Crumble in pieces of cheese and serve.

LABNEH & PISTACHIO BALLS WITH STRAWBERRY FATTOUSH

SERVES
4

Labneh is a strained yogurt from the Middle East, which has a very sour taste. Labneh is one of the oldest dairy products made by humans, first made around 7,500 years ago as a source of fat and protein. Yogurt was widely consumed because the majority of the population was lactose intolerant – and the bacteria used to make yogurt contains lactase, the enzyme that helps to break down lactose in milk into simple sugars, making it easier to digest. Because labneh is so sour, this recipe has quite a lot of honey, so taste the cheese and add the honey gradually to your taste.

In a mixing bowl combine the labneh, almond milk, honey, sumac and a pinch of salt and pepper. Labneh is very sour; we really like that taste, but you can tone it down with honey, olive oil and salt if you find it too strong.

Blitz the pistachios and almonds to a coarse texture in a blender. Tip onto a baking tray or large plate.

Halve the cucumber lengthways. (Because we often make this dish for people's lunches that are served several hours later, we like to use a small spoon to remove the watery core of the cucumber, preserving the crunch of the salad. If you're serving immediately, you may want to keep the core.)

Cut the cumber diagonally into thin slices the same size as the strawberries. Toss the cucumber in a pinch of salt and the poppy

300g labneh

40ml raw almond milk

3 tablespoons raw honey,
depending on how sour
you want the flavour

1 tablespoon ground sumac

150g shelled pistachios

50g raw almonds

½ cucumber

8 strawberries, thinly sliced

1 tablespoon poppy seeds

6 little gem lettuces

a handful of mint leaves

1 tablespoon good-quality
za'atar

5 tablespoons cold-pressed
extra virgin olive oil

juice of 1 lemon

sea salt and freshly ground
black pepper

Carrot, cumin and raisin
flatbreads (see the
introduction of the carrot
salad on page 58), to serve

seeds and place in a colander over the sink until ready to serve
the salad.

Meanwhile, prepare the labneh balls. Using two teaspoons,
gather a spoonful of labneh mix and scrape it into the nuts. Roll
the ball in the nuts to coat and set aside on a clean tray. Allow
around three balls per person.

Thickly slice the gem lettuces into a mixing bowl. Add the
strawberries, cucumber, mint leaves and za'atar, add a pinch of
salt and pepper, olive oil and the lemon juice, toss vigorously and
divide between four plates. Arrange the labneh balls on top of
the salad.

Serve with carrot flatbreads.

BEETROOT SALAD WITH CHILLI & LIME MAYO

SERVES
4

4 beetroot, tops removed,
   washed and peeled

1 small red chilli, finely sliced

a handful of coriander,
   chopped

4 handfuls of lamb's lettuce

FOR THE CHILLI & LIME MAYO

1 free-range egg yolk

½ teaspoon sea salt

120ml vegetable oil

juice of 1 lime

1 teaspoon shiro miso paste

2 garlic cloves, crushed

1cm cube of ginger, peeled
   and grated

3 tablespoons rice vinegar

1 small red chilli, crushed

FOR THE MISO DRESSING

4 tablespoons shiro miso paste

3 tablespoons raw honey

1 tablespoon rice wine vinegar

2 teaspoons mirin (sweet
   rice wine)

We often serve this salad at Karma Cans.
It's super-crunchy and tastes great, but
prepare for beetroot-stained fingers!

First make the mayo. In a large heavy mixing bowl, mix the egg yolk with the salt. Add the miso, garlic and ginger. Pour the oil into a jug or squeeze bottle so you can control how much you pour in at a time.

Drip the oil into the egg drop by drop and slowly whisk in each drop until it has been incorporated before adding the next drop. After a quarter of the oil has been added, pour in a quarter of the lime juice.

Begin adding the oil again, pouring it in a thin constant stream while you whisk the egg. The mayo will gradually thicken. As it gets thick, pour in the rest of the lime juice and the rice vinegar gradually – the mixture will thin and turn paler – then continue adding in the oil until it is all incorporated. Then stir in the chilli.

For the miso dressing, combine all the ingredients together in a bowl and whisk.

Slice the beetroot using a mandoline set to its thinnest setting.

Toss the beetroot with the chilli, coriander and lamb's lettuce in a large bowl. Drizzle over spoonfuls of the miso dressing and the mayo. You may not need all the mayo but it will last for a day in the fridge.

SUMMER COURGETTE SALAD

SERVES
2

1 courgette

3 handfuls of rocket leaves

a handful of baby plum
   tomatoes

1 ripe avocado

juice of 1 lime

1 tablespoon mixed seeds

sea salt and freshly ground
   black pepper

FOR THE DRESSING

4 tablespoons cold-pressed
   extra virgin olive oil

juice of 1 lemon

¾ tablespoon Dijon mustard

1 garlic clove, grated

pinch of salt and freshly
   ground black pepper

This simple salad is perfect either as a
healthy light lunch or a side dish. It has lots
of different textures to play with.

Spiralize or finely julienne the courgette into a large bowl.
Mix with the rocket and tomatoes.

Stone and peel the avocado and cut into chunks. Marinate
the chunks in lime juice, salt and pepper.

Mix the dressing ingredients together.

Add the avocado to the salad bowl and sprinkle the seeds
and dressing on top.

ANCHOVY & TOMATO SALAD

SERVES
6

1kg heritage tomatoes

5 anchovies

a handful of raw samphire

juice of 1 lemon

300g soft, raw milk cheese

pinch of sea salt

FOR THE DRESSING

3 small cherry tomatoes

2 garlic cloves

1 long red chilli

5 tablespoons cold-pressed
   extra virgin olive oil

1 teaspoon raw honey

3 tablespoons sherry
   vinegar

freshly ground black pepper

Samphire is a delicious sea green. It's very
salty and works wonders in this recipe, but
it has a short season, so if you can't find it
any sea green works well.

First make the dressing. Finely chop the cherry tomatoes,
garlic and chilli and mix with the oil into a paste. Stir in the
honey, and add the vinegar and pepper to taste.

Cut the heritage tomatoes into quarters or slices depending
on their size and your preference. Place in a colander over a
bowl, add a pinch of salt and toss. Allow to drain for
25 minutes at room temperature. (Save the liquid in the bowl
to make Gazpacho – see page 28).

Chop the anchovies into little pieces, roughly chop the
samphire and toss in the lemon juice.

Arrange the tomatoes on a large serving plate, tear the
cheese over, sprinkle with anchovies and samphire and
finally pour over the dressing before serving.

SEAWEED SALAD

SERVES 4

50g dried sea vegetable salad (2 packets) or 2 packets mixed frozen seaweed, defrosted

juice of 1 lemon

FOR THE DRESSING

3 tablespoons tahini

½ teaspoon homemade Aioli (see page 157)

1 teaspoon raw cane sugar

1 teaspoon mirin

2 tablespoons nama shoyu or soy sauce

2 tablespoons sesame oil

2 tablespoons rice vinegar

This Japanese salad is riduculously simple, though it seems so impressive. You can add lots of different ingredients – sliced jellyfish, cucumber, lettuce and kelp noodles also work well.

We normally serve this with miso aubergine, raw maki rolls and either this dressing or the sesame dressing on page 156.

If using dried seaweed, soak for 10 minutes in cold water. Drain and squeeze gently; repeat this process a few times to get rid of any excess salt. After each soak, taste the seaweed to test the saltiness of it. When it tastes right, drain and squeeze for a final time.

While the seaweed is soaking, whisk the dressing ingredients vigorously in a bowl until very smooth.

Squeeze the lemon over the top of the seaweed. Toss in the dressing and serve.

CELERIAC SALAD WITH SMOKED FISH

½ large celeriac, cut into thick rectangular wedges

2 large handfuls of rocket leaves

280g cold-smoked fish, to serve

FOR THE DRESSING

1 teaspoon raw honey

1 tablespoon Dijon mustard

2 tablespoons cold-pressed extra virgin olive oil

squeeze of lemon

This salad mixes the nutty sweetness of the celeriac with peppery rocket and the kick of Dijon mustard. We like this with cold-smoked fish (use 70g per person), or with Beetroot Ravioli (page 38) and we often mix Oven-dried Celeriac (page 153) into the salad to add a different texture and flavour.

Ideally, you will need a mandoline or use a very sharp vegetable peeler. Set the mandoline to a thin setting, and thinly slice the celeriac into strips, or use a vegetable peeler. You want the celeriac in wafer-thin ribbons that absorb the dressing.

Toss the celeriac with the rocket in a large bowl. Pour over the dressing and toss to coat the salad. Place the smoked fish on serving plates and add the salad.

SMOKED EEL
SALAD

1 cucumber

2 fennel bulbs

2 red or white endive heads, leaves separated

zest and juice of 1 unwaxed lemon

4 tablespoons cold-pressed extra virgin olive oil

a handful of flat-leaf parsley, chopped

600g good-quality cold-smoked eel fillet

sea salt and freshly ground black pepper

Smoked eel is really delicious and should be regarded as a treat. European eels breed in the Sargasso Sea, which is over 3,500 miles away in the middle of the North Atlantic Ocean. During the rest of the year they live in waterways across Europe and have faced significant threats to their habitat and migratory paths. Happily, measures are being taken to help eels migrate and so their numbers are rising.

Halve the cucumber lengthways and scoop out the seeds with a teaspoon.

Cut the cucumber and fennel finely with a mandoline and put into a salad bowl.

Add the endive leaves to the bowl. Toss together. Add the lemon zest and juice, oil and parsley and season with salt and pepper to taste.

Serve in bowls with the fillet of eel on top.

VIETNAMESE NOODLE SALAD

SERVES 2

2 carrots

a small bunch of rău ram, or use ½ mint ½ coriander

a small bunch of ngò ôm, or if you cannot find this add ¼ teaspoon cumin

1 endive head

1 butterhead lettuce

1 packet (250g) kelp noodles

12 ama-ebi shrimp (sweet prawns)

½ cucumber

2 spring onions

2 perilla or shiso leaves

2 small handfuls of beansprouts

4 tablespoons dried shallot (shop-bought or sliced thinly and dehydrated for 3 hours)

4 tablespoons peanuts

FOR THE DRESSING

2½ tablespoons fish sauce

1 tablespoon raw honey

juice of 1 lime

1 teaspoon rice vinegar

This Vietnamese noodle salad is a fresh mixture of kelp noodles and vegetables with a sour dressing and crunchy toppings. We like to serve this with all the elements separated so when you eat it you can see all the different parts of the dish. We've added lots of fresh Vietnamese flavours here, however we've also added crunchy endive leaves, which is bitter and counters the sweetness of the dressing, carrots, onions and noodles.

Spiralize the carrot. Roughly chop the herbs. Pick the endive leaves and separate out the lettuce leaves. Soak the kelp noodles in cold water for 10 minutes, then drain. Peel the ama-ebi shrimp and devein. Halve the cucumber lengthways, remove the seeds then julienne (cut into thin matchsticks). Cut the spring onions lengthways into quarters then shred thinly.

Mix all the dressing ingredients together. Place a handful of noodles into the centre of two separate bowls. Arrange the other vegetables around the noodles: the carrot, lettuce, endive, cucumber, beansprouts, leaves and the herbs and spring onions. Top the noodles with the ama-ebi and pour over the dressing. Garnish with the shallot and peanuts and serve.

MUSSELS, SEAWEED & KELP NOODLE SALAD

SERVES 4

1kg extremely fresh, cleaned mussels, beards removed

1 red chilli

3 garlic cloves

2 unwaxed lemons

10 nori sheets

150g raw butter (unsalted), softened

1 bunch of radishes, with the leaves on

50g dried sea vegetable salad

1 packet (250g) kelp noodles, soaked in cold water for 10 minutes, then drained

1 teaspoon fresh ground black pepper

2 tablespoons cold-pressed extra virgin olive oil

pinch of salt

In the south of France fresh mussels picked that day are eaten raw with a little lemon and salt, similar to oysters. Be sure to remove the beards and clean them thoroughly before you serve them. This dish tastes like the sea, with seaweed butter, fresh seaweed and seafood – it's a celebration of the marine elements.

The mussels should be alive when you buy them and very fresh. Their shells should close tightly when tapped, discard any that remain open. Use a knife to pry open the shell and then rinse out any grit around the mussel. Store in the fridge and keep damp.

Finely mince the chilli and the garlic together and set aside. Zest and juice the lemons and set aside.

Blitz the nori sheets in a food processor for 30 seconds until they form a fine powder, then add the butter to the blender creating a deep green butter. Add the garlic and chilli and pulse for 10 seconds until incorporated.

Now melt the butter at 35°C until it just becomes liquid. Clean the radishes and mandoline the bulbs on the thinnest setting. Keep the leaves to add to the salad.

Soak the sea vegetables in cold water for 10 minutes to reduce their saltiness. In a large bowl toss the sea greens, noodles and the radish slices and leaves with half the lemon juice.

Split the noodle mixture between four small bowls and lay a quarter of the raw open mussels over each bowl, add a tiny pinch of salt and pepper and a drop of lemon juice to each mussel, drizzle over the olive oil, before spooning over the seaweed butter dressing.

CHEESE & HAM PIZZA

SERVES 4

FOR THE PIZZA BASE

kernels of 2 corn on the cob

2 courgettes, roughly chopped

2 handfuls of raw cashews

1 teaspoon ground ginger

1 teaspoon ground cumin

1 teaspoon ground paprika

2 tablespoons cold-pressed extra virgin olive oil

pinch of sea salt and freshly ground black pepper

450ml raw tomato sauce (see page 89)

4 slices San Daniele cured ham

300g soft, raw cheese (we like Waterloo)

a handful of wild rocket leaves

2 tablespoons cold-pressed extra virgin olive oil

zest of 2 unwaxed lemons

This is a great one to make when people are coming over because you can get the base ready a day in advance and store it in an airtight container so that when everyone arrives you just need to assemble it!

Pulse the sweetcorn, courgette and cashews together in a blender or food processor until smooth, then add the rest of the ingredients. If the mixture is not blending well, add a small amount of water to help the process.

When the mixture is smooth, cover a tray with baking parchment and pour the mixture onto it in the chosen pizza base shape you want. (Depending on the size of your dehydrator you may be able to make 2 larger pizza bases, but in our dehydrator we couldn't fit in 2 large pizza bases so we made 4 small ones.) Leave to dehydrate in the oven on its lowest setting or in a dehydrator at 37°C overnight.

Lay the pizza bases out and cover with spoonfuls of the tomato sauce.

Tear the ham and cheese into strips and sprinkle over each base. Top with rocket leaves, olive oil and lemon zest.

FRESH TOMATO NOODLES

SERVES
2-3

1 packet (250g) kelp
  noodles, soaked in cold
  water for 10 minutes

FOR THE TOMATO SAUCE

650g fresh cherry tomatoes

juice of 1 lemon

2 garlic cloves

a handful of fresh basil

1½ small chillies

2 teaspoons white wine
  vinegar

1 teaspoon grated parmesan

3 tablespoons cold-pressed
  extra virgin olive oil

1 teaspoon sea salt

1 teaspoon freshly ground
  pepper

FOR THE TOPPING

a handful of pine nuts or
  mixed seeds

1 teaspoon cold-pressed
  extra virgin olive oil

½ garlic clove

This fresh, light tomato sauce is perfect for a summer
evening. The flavours are punchy and strong and go well
with any salad. It can be served with kelp noodles or, if you
prefer, courgetti (spiralized or grated courgette).

Slice the cherry tomatoes in half and leave them in a sieve
to drain over the sink while you prepare the other
ingredients. This will remove some of the liquid so the
sauce is not too watery.

For the sauce, in a blender pulse the lemon juice, garlic,
basil, chillies, vinegar, parmesan and olive oil together. Once
the ingredients are puréed, add the cherry tomatoes, salt and
pepper and blitz for 10 seconds. You don't want the tomatoes
to be completely puréed.

Put the pine nuts or seeds in a bowl. Mix in the olive oil and
grated garlic. If you want, crush the nuts with a pestle and
mortar to break them up.

Drain the kelp noodles and place in a bowl. Pour the sauce
over the noodles and then add the crunchy seeds as a
garnish for great texture. If you have any leftover basil, use a
few leaves to garnish.

CELERIAC PASTA & PESTO

SERVES 2

1 celeriac, cut into thick
  rectangular wedges

30g raw hazelnuts

30g aged parmesan
  (parmigiano reggiano),
  sliced thinly

FOR THE PESTO

1 garlic clove

110ml cold-pressed extra
  virgin olive oil

a large handful of basil

a handful of very fresh
  watercress

50g aged parmesan
  (parmigiano reggiano),
  crumbled

50g pine nuts

squeeze of lemon

zest of ½ unwaxed lemon

sea salt and freshly ground
  black pepper, to taste

Aged cheese like parmesan has been allowed
to ferment for around two years, a process
that breaks down most of the lactose in
the milk solids as the bacteria that grow on
the cheese are able to produce the enzyme
lactase which helps to convert lactose into
simple sugars. This means that if you have
a lactose intolerance, parmesan could be a
great option for you. It is generally agreed
by the FSA and, in the USA, the FDA that raw
milk hard cheeses have very low levels of
E. coli and salmonella because the acidity
of the cheese kills these types of harmful
pathogens, so this is another good reason to
use parmesan in your dishes.

Put the garlic in a blender with a little of the oil and a tiny bit of
salt and blend until a paste is formed.

Add the green leaves (if desired all basil can be used but
watercress bulks it out) and blend for a few seconds. Add some
more olive oil.

Add the cheese and pine nuts and more oil and blend. Taste
at this stage – if it's quite oily add some lemon juice, if dry
add more oil. Blend and then season with lemon zest, salt and
pepper. (You can store in the fridge, covered in a layer of oil for
up to a week.)

Spiralize the celeriac into spaghetti. Toss in the pesto and
season with salt and pepper. Divide between two bowls and top
with hazelnuts and parmesan.

AVOCADO PESTO

You had better trust us! You're about to fall down an avocado rabbit hole. We had some dairy-free clients who ordered our pesto, so we replaced the parmesan cheese with avocado. It was great! Serve with courgetti.

300g walnuts

2 garlic cloves

½ red chilli

1 teaspoon black peppercorns

1½ teaspoons sea salt

5 tablespoons cold-pressed extra virgin olive oil

2 large handfuls of basil leaves

1 tablespoon lemon juice

½ ripe avocado, peeled

First blend the walnuts in a food processor for 30 seconds.

Grate or crush the garlic and chilli so that it's super-fine; the last thing you want is a lump of either in your mouth. Grind the peppercorns – we always grind our pepper fresh each morning so it retains its flavour. Make sure you grind the peppercorns super-fine, like the garlic.

Add the salt, garlic, chilli, pepper, olive oil, basil leaves and lemon juice to the food processor. Blitz for 4 minutes, add the avocado and a little lemon juice to the pesto and blend for a further minute. If it's looking lumpy or dry (rolling around the blender in a ball), drizzle in a bit more olive oil until the consistency is very smooth.

ALMOND PESTO

At different stages of the game we've tried cooked and raw nuts for pesto, and raw gives a smooth texture, lighter flavour and doesn't dull the brilliant green colour. Serve with courgetti, broccoli spaghetti (made from broccoli stalks), Cauliflower Rice (see page 155) or Celeriac Pasta (page 90).

200g raw almonds

2 garlic cloves

½ mild green chilli, deseeded

1 teaspoon black peppercorns

½ teaspoon salt

5 tablespoons olive oil

2 large handfuls of basil leaves

½ teaspoon lemon juice

50g aged parmesan (parmigiano reggiano), grated

First blend the almonds in a food processor until smooth.

Grate or crush the garlic so that it's super-fine. Grate the chilli. Grind the peppercorns until really fine.

Add the salt, garlic, chilli, pepper, olive oil, basil leaves and lemon juice to the food processor. Blitz the pesto for 4 minutes. Add the parmesan. If it's looking lumpy or dry (rolling around the blender in a ball), drizzle in a bit more olive oil until the consistency is very smooth.

Once the parmesan has been added try not to blend for more than 5 minutes, as the heat of the processing can begin to melt the cheese.

CAULIFLOWER TABBOULEH

SERVES 4

2 medium garlic cloves,
   grated

1cm cube fresh ginger,
   peeled and grated

1 small mild green chilli,
   deseeded and finely
   chopped

100ml cold-pressed extra
   virgin olive oil

zest and juice of 2½
   unwaxed lemons

1 recipe Cauliflower Rice
   (page 155)

2 large bunches of flat-leaf
   parsley

¼ bunch coriander

a small bunch of mint

sea salt and freshly ground
   black pepper

The cauliflower rice absorbs all the flavour
from the parsley, garlic and olive oil to
make a punchy and filling salad.

Mix the garlic with the ginger and chilli in a deep salad bowl.
Add the oil and lemon juice and mix together thoroughly. Add
the cauliflower rice and toss.

Grip the parsley in manageable handfuls, chop off and discard
the very thick, tough parts of the stalks, but keep the tender
upper stalk. Begin very finely chopping the parsley, from the
stalks to the leaves, moving the knife in quick motions up and
down. Try to cut as finely as possible first time around, so you
don't have to chop it again, which bruises the leaves.

Repeat with the coriander.

Pick the mint leaves off the stalks. If you're feeling particularly
lazy you could skip this, but the stalks are pretty tough. Gather
the mint up into a compact handful and finely chop.

Toss the herbs into the bowl with the cauliflower and dressing
and mix through before serving. Season with salt and pepper.

TROUT CEVICHE

1 trout fillet

4 spring onions, finely sliced

a very small handful of coriander, finely chopped

a very small handful of basil, finely chopped

1 tablespoon finely sliced fennel bulb

zest and juice of 1 unwaxed lemon

½ head broccoli

cold-pressed extra virgin olive oil

sea salt and freshly ground black pepper

FOR THE DRESSING

2 tablepoons cider vinegar

4 tablespoons cold-pressed extra virgin olive oil

¼ chilli, finely chopped

1 small garlic clove, grated

1 teaspoon raw honey

Trout is not a fish usually used for ceviche, but we think it's amazing. Like salmon it's an oily fish, and it has a similar flavour and texture, the only difference being a lower fat content, giving it a slightly lighter taste. It is one of the most sustainable farmed fish on the market, farmed in inland pools, which is better for the environment as the fish don't contaminate the rivers or seas, and often the water is carefully managed and recycled into the tanks, with the waste used as fertiliser for surrounding farms. Ask your fishmonger to fillet the trout for you and remove all the small bones and skin.

Cut the trout fillet into strips lengthways, trying to cut where the grain of the fish meets, then cut the strips into triangular chunks at odd angles (see page 101). Place in a bowl, season with salt and pepper, and add the spring onion, chopped herbs, fennel and lemon zest.

Don't add the lemon juice yet, as this starts off the curing process, and to keep the soft texture of the trout it's better to wait until about 10 minutes before you want to eat it.

Cut the broccoli into tiny florets – as small as you can – and cut the stalk into even-sized very small cubes. Cut the lemon in half, add a squeeze of juice from the one of the halves, then season with salt and a little olive oil.

For the dressing, mix all the ingredients together. Add 1½ teaspoons of dressing to the finely sliced spring onion to pickle it a little, then arrange on your plate, broccoli on the bottom, trout on top and spoonfuls of spring onion around the trout. Keep in the fridge.

Ten minutes before you eat, squeeze the lemon onto the trout and dress the salad.

SALMON TARTARE

SERVES
2

¼ side of salmon, skinned
   and boned

juice of 1 lemon

3 tablespoons cold-pressed
   extra virgin olive oil

1 teaspoon peeled and
   grated ginger

½ white onion, finely
   chopped

2 tablespoons capers, finely
   chopped

a small handful of flat-leaf
   parsley, finely chopped

a small handful of rocket
   leaves, chopped

sea salt

FOR THE SALAD

1 cucumber

4 handfuls of watercress

1 recipe Simple Lemon
   Dressing (see page 156)

We all know that fish is good for brain
development and is packed with
protein. This tasty tartare is perfect for
a quick light lunch or dinner.

Finely chop the salmon, first into strips and then finely chop
into very small cubes. This way, you only cut once, rather than
mashing it up or mincing it with the knife.

Add the lemon juice, olive oil, ginger, onion, capers and parsley
and mix well. Add salt to taste. Divide and shape into two balls.

Using a vegetable peeler, mandoline or a spiralizer, shave the
cucumbers lengthways into ribbons. Put the cucumber and
watercress in a bowl and toss in the dressing.

Divide the salad between two plates and top with the salmon.

SALMON CEVICHE

SERVES 4

½ side of salmon, skinned and boned

a bunch of fresh coriander (reserve a few leaves for garnish), finely chopped – particularly the stalks

5 spring onions, finely sliced

¼ fennel bulb, finely chopped

zest and juice of 2 limes

zest and juice of 1 unwaxed lemon

100ml cold-pressed extra virgin olive oil

4 Spicy Tacos (see page 150)

sea salt and freshly ground black pepper

This is a very popular dish at Karma Cans. For us the most important part is the cutting of the fish. We always use fillet cut from the head end of the fish, which is fattier and softer than the tail end. When you look at the fish you'll notice that the pink flesh is interlaced by white zigzag lines of white fat and when you cut the fish into strips it's good to cut along the dips in the zigzag patterns. Essentially, you're cutting along the natural seams of the fish. When it comes to cutting the fish into cubes, we like to make the pieces irregular shapes, increasing the surface area of the chunks so each piece gets coated with as much flavour as possible.

Remove the skin from the salmon, cut the fillet lengthways, along the natural gradients of the fish, then cut the strips into chunks. If you cut the fish at odd angles it exposes the lines of fat through the salmon and creates a more interesting texture. Transfer to a bowl.

Mix the finely chopped coriander, spring onion and fennel through the fish.

Add 1 teaspoon of salt, the zest, citrus and olive oil.

About 10 minutes before serving add the citrus juice, toss through and let it marinate.

Just before serving, check the seasoning. Crack a taco over the each portion and garnish with a few coriander leaves.

SALMON
CHIRASHI

½ side of salmon, skinned
and boned

7.5cm knob of peeled ginger

2 large garlic cloves

½ lime

2 handfuls of rocket leaves,
finely chopped

a small bunch of coriander,
finely chopped

a small bunch of basil, finely
chopped

4 sheets nori

3 tablespoons black sesame
seeds

3 tablespoons puffed rice,
optional

Cauliflower Rice (see page
155), to serve

4 shiso leaves

4 mizuna leaves

FOR THE DRESSING

3 tablespoons mirin

2 tablespoons nama shoyu or
soy sauce

2.5cm knob of peeled ginger

1 garlic clove, crushed

2 tablespoons raw honey

¼ tablespoon fish sauce

1 teaspoon shiro miso paste

1 tablespoon rapeseed oil

squeeze of lime

'Chirashi' means scattered in Japanese and usually refers
to a bowl of rice topped with vegetables and sashimi; in
other words, sort of an unstructured home-style sushi. Here
we make it with salmon, ginger, rocket, coriander and basil,
topped with a mirin-soy dressing on sheets of nori. The
puffed rice is optional as it's not strictly raw. Serve this over
Cauliflower Rice (see page 155) with shiso leaves and fresh
mizuna leaves.

First make the dressing. Combine all the ingredients in a
blender and blitz for 30 seconds.

Chop the salmon into very small cubes. Transfer to a bowl.

Grate the ginger and garlic and add to the salmon, squeeze
the lime and the stringy remainder of the ginger root over
the salmon.

Add the rocket, coriander and basil to the fish. Pour in the
dressing and toss through. Divide into four balls.

Lay the nori on four plates. Top with cauliflower rice and the
shiso and mizuna leaves. Add a scoop of chirashi to each and
scatter with black sesame seeds and puffed rice.

SALMON POKE

SERVES 4

This is essentially cubes of raw tuna, marlin or salmon over rice, topped with a soy-based dressing and fish roe. Here we've made it with fresh seaweed, salmon roe and salmon. Go for wild Alaskan salmon if you can find it, a sustainable fish farmed one if not. Alaska's wild salmon fisheries are some of the most sustainable in the world with fishing closely managed. Choose a salmon fillet from the head end; it has a higher fat content and is softer than the tail end.

½ side of salmon (from the head end), skinned

55g (1 packet) mixed dried seaweed salad

4 tablespoons sesame seeds

2 thumb-sized pieces of ginger, grated

4 sheets of nori

2 ripe avocados, stoned, peeled and sliced lengthways

100g Tobiko or salmon roe

4 tablespoons bonito flakes

1 red pepper, julienned

First make the crackers. Grate the carrot, soak the seaweed in water for 10 minutes and drain. In a bowl mix the miso, sugar and oil and add the grated carrot, seaweed, ginger, bonito flakes and puffred rice. Divide into rectangles, about 4cm by 2cm long, flatten out on a wire rack and put in the oven or dehydrator at 37°C for 6–8 hours, flipping halfway through. You could store these up to 4 days in a an airtight container.

For the rice, mix together the rice vinegar, sugar and salt and toss the cauliflower rice in it.

For the onion, mix the onion and the rice vinegar, sugar and salt and set aside in a separate bowl.

FOR THE CRACKERS

100g carrot

150g mixed dried seaweed
salad

2 tablespoons shiro miso
paste

3 tablespoons raw cane
sugar

2 tablespoons cold pressed
rapeseed oil

5g grated ginger

10g bonito flakes

20g puffed rice, optional

FOR THE RICE

6 tablespoons rice vinegar

2 tablespoons raw cane
sugar

2 teaspoons salt

1 Cauliflower Rice Recipe
(see page 155)

FOR THE ONION

1 small onion, finely sliced

1½ tablespoons rice
vinegar

2 teaspoons raw cane
sugar

½ teaspoon sea salt

FOR THE DRESSING

2 tablespoons sesame oil

4 tablespoons nama shoyu
or soy sauce

1 tablespoon raw honey

1 tablespoon mirin

½ tablespoon rice vinegar

juice of 1½ limes

Cut the salmon into strips along the grain of the fish where the natural divides in the fillet are. Once in strips cut into large even-sized cubes (we like them 2cm, but if you're serving to people who are less sure on fish than you are, perhaps cut the cubes a little smaller so the surface area of the fish is increased and the taste of the dressing is more apparent.) Set aside in a bowl in the fridge while you make the rest of the dish.

Soak the dried seaweed in water for 10 minutes, then drain, Combine the dressing ingredients together.

Remove the fish from the fridge, toss with half the dressing, the seaweed, sesame seeds and the ginger.

Lay a sheet of nori on the bottom of four shallow bowls, add a few scoops of rice, then add a quarter of the fish to each bowl. Place the avocado slices next to the fish, then finish with a scoop of salmon roe, a few bonito flakes, the pepper slices and finally the rest of the dressing.

Serve with the seaweed crackers.

SEA BASS
CEVICHE

2 whole fillets of sea bass
(ask your fishmonger to
fillet, skin and debone
your fish)

1 teaspoon sea salt

½ fennel bulb

1 celery stalk

a handful of turnip leaves (or
use butterhead lettuce)

a small handful of coriander

few sprigs of flat-leaf
parsley

zest and juice of 2 unwaxed
lemons

5 tablespoons cold-pressed
olive oil

¼ garlic clove, crushed

freshly ground black pepper

This ceviche is all about the cutting of
the fish. The fish needs to be in 3cm long
triangular pieces, with angled edges.

Cut the sea bass lengthways into 3cm thick strips. Cut
diagonally one way then diagonally the other way to create
uneven triangles. Place in a bowl and add the salt.

Cut the leafy fronds off the fennel and chop them, then slice the
fennel as finely as you can. Finely chop the celery. Wash and tear
up the turnip or lettuce leaves.

Chop the coriander and parsley.

Mix the lemon zest and juice with the oil, crushed garlic, herbs,
fennel and celery, then add to the sea bass.

Serve with the torn leaves tossed through the ceviche and
freshly ground black pepper.

TUNA TATAKI

SERVES
4

350g tuna (buy a whole piece
from the head end of the
tuna, rather than fillets)

juice of 2 limes, zest of 1

1½ heads of broccoli

2 tablespoons sesame oil

5cm knob of ginger, peeled
and grated

4 small, very ripe cherry
tomatoes, finely chopped

1 red pepper, finely chopped

1 long red chilli, finely
chopped

sea salt and freshly ground
black pepper

FOR THE DRESSING

3 tablespoons nama shoyu or
soy sauce

2 tablespoons water

2 tablespoons raw honey

2 tablespoons finely chopped
or grated ginger

1 garlic clove, crushed

1 chilli, finely chopped

Some species of tuna are incredibly
endangered so it's important not to buy
bluefin tuna, but skipjack and big eye
tuna are less endangered. The texture and
flavour of raw tuna is amazing, and it's
worth getting a whole piece rather than a
small fillet or slice because it's easer to cut.

Cut the tuna into 4 long triangular pieces, sprinkle over half the
lime zest and half the juice and salt. Wrap in clingfilm and freeze
for 20 minutes.

Meanwhile, cut the broccoli into tiny florets and cut the stalk
into tiny cubes. Dress with the juice of half a lime, 1 tablespoon
sesame oil and a pinch of salt and pepper. Set aside.

In a separate bowl, mix the ginger, tomatoes, pepper and chilli
with the juice of half a lime and 1 tablespoon of the sesame oil.

Combine all the ingredients for the dressing. Remove the tuna
pieces from the freezer, cut each one into medium slices, arrange
on a plate and spoon over the chopped tomatoes, pepper and
chilli. Add the broccoli and pour the dressing over the top.

PAD THAI

SERVES
2

1 packet (250g) of kelp noodles

a handful of coriander leaves

2 tablespoons dried peanuts (dehydrated for 3 hours), roughly ground

2 large handfuls of beansprouts

1 carrot, spiralized into spaghetti-like curls

3 tablespoons small dried shrimp

1 teaspoon dried garlic flakes (shop-bought or dehyrated in very thin slices for 3 hours)

1 tablespoon dried shallots (shop-bought or dehyrated in very thin slices for 3 hours)

1 lime, cut into wedges

FOR THE DRESSING

30g raw cane sugar

60g dried peanuts (dehydrated for 3 hours), reserving half for garnish

1 teaspoon fermented chilli bean paste

50ml tamarind water

50ml fish sauce

We make this for our customers at Karma Cans quite frequently and it's always very popular. Dehydrating the peanuts gives the dish a stronger flavour. We also love kelp noodles, they're so crunchy and incredibly low in fat and calories – great!

First make the dressing. Grind half the dehydrated peanuts with the sugar using a pestle and mortar. Grind in the chilli paste. Gradually add the tamarind water and fish sauce and keep grinding to fully combine the ingredients. Set aside in a large bowl.

Soak the kelp noodles in cold water for 10 minutes. Pick the coriander leaves off the stalks, then finely chop the stalks.

Drain the kelp noodles and toss in the large bowl containing the dressing, then toss in the beansprouts, carrot and coriander stalks. Finally toss in the dried shrimp.

Divide between two plates and top each portion with the remaining peanuts, dried garlic, dried shallot and coriander leaves and a couple of lime wedges.

BEEF TACOS

SERVES
4

200g organic, aged sirloin
  steak

1 avocado, stoned and peeled

5 tablespoons cold-pressed
  extra virgin olive oil

2 limes

1 really fresh corn on the cob

1 teaspoon raw cane sugar

2 teaspoons smoked paprika

1 teaspoon ground coriander

1 teaspoon ground ginger

4 very small red onions
  (curry onions), finely sliced
  lengthways

1 red pepper, diced small

a small handful of fresh
  coriander, leaves picked

8 Spicy Tacos (see page 150)

sea salt and freshly ground
  pepper

These are really delicious as they are made
from whole cuts of lean sirloin. We've
suggested only 50g of beef per person
which to us is ample.

Freeze the meat for 1 hour, wrapped in baking parchment.

Blend the avocado into a smooth paste in a food processor,
with 1 tablespoon of oil, a pinch of salt and the juice from half
a lime. Set aside.

Stand the corn on the cob upright on a board. Cut the kernels
off the cob with a sharp knife – try to cut down the cob so
they come off in complete slices.

Remove the meat from the freezer and slice it into strips as
thinly as you can.

Juice the remaining limes into a bowl. Drop the strips of meat
into the lime juice, toss for 30 seconds then remove and add a
little salt and pepper and 1 tablespoon of olive oil.

Mix 1 teaspoon of salt, the sugar, remaining oil, paprika,
ground coriander and ginger into the lime juice to make
a dressing.

Now begin assembling the tacos. Spoon a small amount of
avocado onto the base of each taco and spread it across the
taco then pile on the corn, onion, pepper, finally the strips of
beef and the coriander leaves. Spoon over a little dressing
onto each taco and serve.

JUNIPER HOME-CURED DUCK

SERVES 2

2 duck breasts

750g coarse sea salt

350g raw cane sugar

8 juniper berries, crushed

2 rosemary sprigs

YOU WILL NEED

1 non-metallic container large enough for the curing mixture and the duck breasts

2 metal hooks

2 linen tea towels or muslin cloths

1 small bowl or tray that fits on a shelf of your fridge door

The first step in curing the duck, as with curing all meat, is to draw out the water using salt and sugar, and then air-dry it in a cool place. This takes 8 days.

Pat the duck breasts dry with kitchen paper. Mix the salt and sugar with the juniper and rosemary and pour half of the curing mixture in the bottom of the container. Place the duck breasts on top, and pour over the rest of the mixture. Leave, uncovered, in the fridge for 2 days.

Remove the container from the fridge and scrape off the salt mixture. Wrap each breast in a tea towel or muslin, tie a knot in the top, then slip the hooks through the material under the knot and hook the duck parcels onto a shelf in the door of your fridge. Place a small bowl or tray underneath to catch any drips. Leave for 6 days.

CURED DUCK SALAD WITH FIGS & CHEESE

SERVES
4

2 home-cured duck breasts
(see page 113)

a handful of rocket leaves

a handful of baby sorrel
leaves

4 tablespoons pine nuts

4 fresh ripe figs, quartered

100g Stichelton cheese or
any raw milk blue cheese

FOR THE DRESSING

16 fresh blackberries

4 tablespoons balsamic or
red wine vinegar

6 tablespoons cold-pressed
extra virgin olive oil

2 tablespoons raw honey

This is a gorgeous salad featuring thinly
sliced duck, blackberries and figs and
Stichelton cheese served over rocket
and sorrel leaves.

Slice the duck breast as thinly as possible (about the thickness
of sliced ham).

For the dressing, blitz half the blackberries in a blender, sieve
and beat together with the other ingredients.

Arrange the rocket and sorrel leaves on a plate, then layer the
duck slices over the top.

Sprinkle over the pine nuts, fig quarters and remaining
blackberries.

Finally crumble over tiny pieces of cheese and serve with
the dressing.

BAVETTE WITH TOMATOES & PEPPERS

SERVES
2

2 good-quality, organic
    bavette steaks

1½ ripe beefsteak tomatoes

1½ red peppers, deseeded

1 garlic clove

4 tablespoons raw almonds

zest of 1½ unwaxed lemons
    and 1 lemon for squeezing

7 tablespoons cold-pressed
    extra virgin olive oil

sea salt and freshly ground
    black pepper

Get ready for an arm workout here, you need to really beat this bavette until you can almost see through it. You will be well rewarded though!

Remove the steak from the fridge so it can come to room temperature.

Finely chop the tomatoes, peppers, garlic and almonds and tip into a salad bowl. Add one-third of the lemon zest, 4 tablespoons of olive oil, a squeeze of lemon and pinch of salt.

Now move on to the steaks. Place them on a sheet of baking parchment, then place another layer of parchment on top, making a sandwich. Take a large metal spoon or meat mallet and beat the steaks to a thickness of 1cm. Peel back the top layer of paper, sprinkle a large pinch of salt onto the steaks, and then add 1 tablespoon of the olive oil and the rest of the lemon zest. Try to sprinkle the lemon zest evenly so that as you hit the meat, the oils are released. Replace the top layer of paper and continue to beat the steaks for about 20 seconds. Peel back the paper gently, cut each steak into 5 odd-shaped triangles and separate them, sprinkle over the juice of half a lemon and replace the paper.

Now beat the steak again but gently this time, as the meat will be quite thin and delicate and you don't want holes. When the meat is as thin as you can get it without breaking (2mm), pull up the parchment sheet gently and arrange the steak on a clean plate. Top each piece with a spoonful of the tomato and pepper mixture, a squeeze of lemon and a few drops of olive oil. Add a little salt and pepper just before serving.

BEEF TARTARE & SLAW

SERVES 4

A crunchy slaw is the perfect partner to this spicy tartare.

400g good-quality, organic, aged beef, either fillet or rump steak

3 curry onions (very small red onions)

½ teaspoon ground cumin

½ teaspoon ground coriander

1 garlic clove, crushed

2 thumb-sized pieces of ginger, peeled and grated

4 tablespoons dried peanuts (dehydrated for 3 hours), roughly ground

½ teaspoon sea salt

½ teaspoon raw cane sugar

1 tablespoon dried garlic flakes (shop-bought or dehydrated in very thin slices for 3 hours)

2 tablespoons dried shallot (shop-bought or dehydrated in very thin slices for 3 hours)

1 small handful of basil leaves, torn

FOR THE SLAW

½ large red cabbage or a whole small one

1 radicchio

1 small bunch of Thai basil

Freeze the beef for 30 minutes, wrapped tightly in clingfilm.

Meanwhile prepare the slaw and the dressings. Cut the red cabbage lengthways into thick wedges and remove the thick core. Then set the mandoline onto its thinnest setting and mandoline the cabbage into very thin slices. Cut the radicchio in half and slice into very thin slices.

Chop the basils and coriander by starting at the stalks, gripping tightly together and chopping finely, when you get to the leaves, chop through only one time roughly to avoid bruising. Pick the mint off the stalks, bunch up and chop very roughly or even leave whole.

In a large bowl (big enough to fit the whole salad in), make the slaw dressing by combing lime juice, the fish sauce and sugar,

1 very small bunch of basil

1 large bunch of coriander

1 small bunch of mint

FOR THE SLAW DRESSING

1 tablespoon fish sauce

½ lime

1 teaspoon raw cane sugar

FOR THE DRESSING

juice of 2 limes

3 tablespoons fish sauce

2 tablespoons sesame oil

1 tablespoon raw cane sugar

mixing vigorously until the sugar is dissolved. Toss in the red cabbage, radicchio and all the herbs. The salad should be very lightly dressed at this point. Set aside in the fridge while you make the tartare.

Bring the meat out of the freezer, cut into long 1cm-thick strips, then dice into 1cm cubes. Cover with baking parchment and chill in the fridge.

Combine the dressing ingredients in a bowl. Using either a mandoline or a knife, finely slice the small curry onions and add to the dressing. Add the cumin, coriander, crushed garlic and grated ginger to the dressing as well. Using a pestle and mortar, pound the peanuts with the salt and sugar.

Remove the meat from the fridge and toss through with the dressing. Arrange the slaw across a large plate, pouring over any dressing left in the bowl. Add the cubes of tartare over the top, along with any dressing, sprinkle over the dried garlic and shallot, and the salt and sugar peanuts. Finally add the torn basil leaves and serve.

BEEF & HORSERADISH SANDWICH WITH AIOLI

MAKES
4
SANDWICHES

150g celeriac, peeled

zest and juice of 1 unwaxed
    lemon

3 spring onions, finely sliced

2 tablespoons cold-pressed
    extra virgin olive oil

½ tablespoon cider vinegar

100g horseradish, grated

1 garlic clove, crushed or
    grated

80ml Aioli (see page 157)

2 tablespoons Dijon mustard

280g good-quality, organic
    bavette steak

2 handfuls of rocket leaves

sea salt and freshly ground
    black pepper

FOR THE RAW SEED BREAD

250g pumpkin seeds, ground
    into flour

½ teaspoon salt

½ teaspoon cayenne pepper

35g flax seeds

1 red pepper, deseeded

2 tablespoons nutritional
    yeast

40g tahini

½ teaspoon ground black
    pepper

This seed bread is great for all kinds
of sandwiches and it makes a great
breakfast base too.

For the seed bread, put all ingredients in a food processor with
110ml water and blend until smooth. Spread the mixture thinly
on a sheet of baking parchment and dehydrate for 6–8 hours in
your oven or dehydrator at 37°C or overnight if still wet. Remove
and cut into 8 pieces.

Julienne the celeriac on a mandoline or use a grater or spiralizer
to create fine strips. Toss the spring onions in 1 tablespoon olive
oil and the cider vinegar. In a separate bowl, mix together the
horseradish, celeriac, garlic and lemon zest. Add half the aioli
and the mustard.

Place the steak between two sheets of baking parchment and
beat out as thin as possible with a meat mallet. After a certain
point it will become difficult to go any thinner working the
whole steak, so at this point cut it into 3–5 small triangles.

Dress each triangle with a pinch of salt, a drizzle of olive oil and
a drop of lemon juice.

Put the steak back between the parchment sheets again and
continue to beat until they almost break apart and are as thin as
sliced ham.

Spoon the remaining aioli onto each slice of bread. Place a
few thin slices of steak over. Season with pepper. Top with a
spoonful of the celeriac and horseradish and then finish with
rocket, spring onions and lemon juice before adding the second
slice of bread.

BO TAI CHANH

SERVES
4

Bo tai Chanh is a Vietnamese raw beef salad. Pieces of beef are sliced very very thinly and cured in citrus, served with lightly pickled onions, rau răm (Vietnamese coriander), tía tô (red shiso leaf), and ngò ôm (rice paddy herb).

400g good-quality beef fillet or veal rose fillet

3 limes

1 medium white onion

3 tablespoons rice vinegar

1 tablespoon sugar

1 teaspoon salt

8 red shiso leaves

8 shiso or perilla leaves

1½ bunches rau ram, or a small bunch of mint and of coriander

1 bunch ngo om, or use ¼ teaspoon cumin

3 tablespoons black sesame seed

Start with the toasts as they take the longest. Soak the shrimp in 2 tablespoons of water and the lime juice to rehydrate them slightly and make them more pliable. In a high speed blender, blitz the macadamia nuts to a fine meal. Add the carrot, half the shrimp and all their soaking water and pulse for a few seconds. Add the oil, spices, ginger and sugar and pulse for another 5 seconds – the mixture should be fairly rough. Transfer to a bowl and stir in the rest of the shrimp whole.

Form the mixture into small balls and flatten into thin discs 1cm thick or less, on a baking sheet. Using the lowest setting on your oven or a dehydrater at 37°C, dehydrate for 4–6 hours, flipping half way through the process.

For the beef, freeze the fillet for 20 minutes before you start – this makes it easier to slice. Remove from the freezer and slice

FOR THE BEEF DRESSING

3 tablespoons nama shoyu
   or soy sauce

2 tablespoons sesame oil

1 tablespoon raw cane
   sugar

¼ teaspoon crushed garlic

½ teaspoon peeled and
   grated ginger

FOR THE SHRIMP TOAST

100g small dried shrimp

squeeze of lime

125g macadamia nuts

50g finely grated carrot

1 tablespoon groundnut oil

½ teaspoon ground cumin

½ teaspoon ground
   coriander

1 teaspoon peeled and
   grated ginger

¼ teaspoon raw cane sugar

as thinly as you can – you're aiming for almost paper thinness. Cover with baking parchment and immediately return to the fridge until the other elements are ready.

Juice the limes into a large bowl and set aside. Mandoline or finely slice the onions. Combine the rice vinegar, sugar and salt in a separate bowl, add the onion and toss together.

In a separate bowl, combine the ingredients for the dressing.

Lay the shiso leaves out on a large flat plate. Finely chop the rest of the herbs and arrange over the top of the shiso leaves.

Now remove the meat from the fridge and bathe the slithers in the lime juice for around 1 minute. Remove from the lime and layer in rough folds over the herbs. Dress with the beef dressing. Finish off with the finely sliced onion scattered over each piece of meat.

Serve with the prawn toasts, scooping slices of meat onto each piece of toast.

DESSERTS & DRINKS

APPLE CRUMBLE

2 eating apples

juice of 1 lemon

2 plums, stoned

75g fresh raspberries

3 tablespoons raw honey

whipped raw cream
(optional), to serve

FOR THE TOPPING

beetroot pulp from 1 small
beetroot (juice a beetroot,
reserving the juice for
another purpose)

130g raw almonds

115g raw pecans

30g raw hazelnuts

50g oatmeal

FOR THE SAUCE

50g raw butter

4 tablespoons raw cane
sugar

4 teaspoons ground
cinnamon

½ teaspoon sea salt

¼ teaspoon ground nutmeg

¼ teaspoon ground ginger

This is probably our favourite dessert. The spiced butter sauce with the fruit, crunchy crumble and raw cream is our perfect pudding. And the colour is vivid pink, couldn't be better really!

Quarter the apples, removing the core, then thinly slice or use a mandoline.

Arrange the apples in a spiral in a tart tin or on a flat plate. Squeeze the lemon juice over. Put the plums, raspberries and honey in a blender and blend until very smooth. Sieve the mixture and pour over the apple slices.

Blitz the ingredients for the crunchy topping in a food processor for 30–40 seconds until a rough consistency is achieved, then sprinkle the topping over the fruit as evenly as possible.

For the sauce, melt the butter at 35°C, until just liquid and stir in the sugar, salt and spices. Once they are fully incorporated, drizzle over the top of the crumble.

Serve with whipped raw cream, if liked.

CHILLED CHERRY SOUP WITH NUT CRUNCH

2 oranges

300g cherries, pitted

100ml water

5 tablespoons raw acacia honey

½ teaspoon cardamom seeds

3 fresh figs, quartered

FOR THE YOGURT

480g raw kefir, frozen

1 very ripe banana, frozen

FOR THE NUT CRUNCH

100g raw pecans

35g raw macadamia nuts

1 teaspoon cinnamon

¼ teaspoon ground ginger

25g oatmeal

5g raw butter, melted at 35°C

4 tablespoons raw honey

Chilled fruit soups are very popular in Scandinavia. This is our version, which includes a type of raw yogurt called kefir – it's extremely sour, which we both really like. We've only sweetened it with a banana, but you can add some raw honey into the mix if you would like it sweeter.

First make the yogurt. In a blender, pulse the frozen raw kefir and the banana. This is to aerate the mixture and create a sweeter frozen yogurt. Pulse for a minute until fully incorporated and smooth, pour into a freezer container and refreeze.

Now make the crunch. Pound the nuts roughly using a pestle and mortar, dust with the spices, add the oatmeal, the melted butter and honey and dry in the oven at it's lowest setting or in a dehydrator at 37°C for 6–8 hours. (The crunch will last for a week in a sealed container in the fridge.)

Now prepare the oranges and the soup. Using a small knife, peel and segment the oranges, removing the pith, seeds and all the membrane.

Put the pitted cherries in a blender and blend them until very smooth (around 30 seconds). Sieve the mixture to remove any lumps. Add the water. Sweeten the soup with honey, pound the cardamom using a pestle and mortar and add it to the soup.

Divide the orange segments and fig quarters between 4 small bowls and pour the cherry soup over. Scoop a ball of the frozen kefir over the soup and top with the nut crunch.

FROZEN BANANA LOLLIES

MAKES
20

10 overripe bananas or
20 mini bananas

20 lollipop sticks or flat
bamboo skewers (if they
are for the kids, try to find
skewers with blunt tips, to
avoid any nasty sharp bits
in mouths)

FOR THE TOPPINGS

400g raw chocolate

50g crushed freeze-dried
raspberries

200g crushed pecans

Better than a lollipop, with all the fibre,
vitamins and sugar from a banana,
this is an unprocessed, low-tech way to
make ice cream on a stick. It's a great
recipe for kids to eat and also to make,
plus you can dip these treats in melted
chocolate once they are frozen and then
dip them into all kinds of toppings from
crushed pecans to crushed freeze-dried
raspberries. We suggest making lots…
what's the point in only making two?
You'll run out too fast…

Peel the bananas and cut them in half (if using the larger ones).
Insert a stick into each one. Wrap the lollies individually in
parchment paper or clingfilm. Freeze for at least 2 hours.

Meanwhile, melt the chocolate in a heatproof bowl, either in
the microwave on a low setting or over a saucepan of barely
simmering water. Stir until smooth.

Remove the bananas from the freezer, take off the packaging
and dip into the melted chocolate, then sprinkle on your choice
of toppings, re-wrap and re-freeze for another hour.

BERRY MILLEFEUILLE

SERVES
4

500ml raw cream

50g freeze-dried raspberries

200g strawberries, sliced
thinly

FOR THE 'PASTRY'

300g raw almonds, soaked
for 12 hours

7 tablespoons raw honey

90g raw butter, melted
at 35°C

seeds scraped from
1 vanilla pod

FOR THE FRAMBOISE

1kg frozen raspberries

4 tablespoons raw honey

200ml water

pinch of sea salt

This traditional French dessert is normally made using thin layers of puff pastry, whipped cream or crème patissière and fresh berries. We have substituted a ground almond base for the pastry. Here the star of the show is the raw cream, which has a completely unique flavour. Organic raw milk from a single origin herd has not been homogenised and no antibiotics are included in the cows' routine diet, they only eat grass and herd health is closely monitored, so don't be scared about using it.

For the 'pastry', drain the almonds and blitz in a blender until very smooth. Add the other ingredients, blend for 30 seconds until smooth and sticky. Form into 12 even-sized small rectangles less than 1cm thick on a baking sheet and either oven-dry or dehydrate at 37°C for 24 hours, flipping midway through. They should be slightly crispy and pliable.

For the framboise, put all the ingredients into the blender and pulse for 1 minute until smooth then sieve and chill.

Whip the cream until it just begins to stiffen. Crush up the freeze-dried berries.

Now assemble the dish. Take each 'pastry' rectangle and, using 2 teaspoons, drop small balls of whipped cream onto the bases, or pipe using a piping bag. Sprinkle with crushed freeze-dried berries, top with an overlapping layer of dehydrated strawberries and then drizzle over a little framboise. This makes one base. Gently assemble your four portions by stacking three layered bases, one of top of the other.

AVOCADO & BLACKBERRY RIPPLE ICE CREAM

SERVES
4

3–4 large, very ripe avocados, stoned and peeled

750ml raw almond milk

140g raw honey

¾ teaspoon xantham gum

juice of ½ lemon

300g blackberries, plus extra to decorate

Avocados make amazing ice cream. With ice cream, a quick freezing time helps control the build up of crystals; the quicker the ice cream freezes, the creamier it will be. For this non-dairy ice cream, we've added the all-natural emulsifier, xantham gum, to the recipe, which prevents large crystals forming, resulting in a smooth, creamy texture.

Put the avocados in a blender and blend until very smooth. Gradually add the almond milk, three-quarters of the honey and the xantham gum. Add a squeeze of lemon juice. Stop and taste the mixture – you may need to add a little more honey to get it sweet because, when the mixture freezes, it will taste less sweet, so you want the mixture to be very slightly sweeter than you would like.

If you're using an ice-cream maker, switch it on and get it chilling, pour in the mixture and set the timer for 50 minutes. If you're not using an ice-cream maker, pour the mixture into a freezerproof container and put straight in the freezer for 1½ hours. When the ice cream is almost frozen, tip it back into the blender, blend for 30 seconds, return to the ice-cream maker or the container in the freezer and continue to chill.

Meanwhile, make the blackberry ripple. Clean the blender, blend the blackberries with the remainder of the honey and lemon juice and pass through a sieve.

In the last stage of freezing, swirl the blackberry purée wih a spoon if using the freezer method, or drizzle slowly into the ice-cream maker to make the ripple. As you add the blackberries, the warmth and high sugar content will slow or begin to reverse the freezing process, so advance the timer of the ice-cream maker for 10 minutes. When the paddle can no longer turn, take the ice cream out and either serve immediately or store in the freezer.

FLAPJACK CUPS & ALMOND ICE CREAM

MAKES
6
CUPS

FOR THE ALMOND ICE CREAM

3 large very ripe bananas, frozen for 2 hours

1 litre raw almond milk

140g raw honey

¾ teaspoon xantham gum

juice of ½ lemon

FOR THE FLAPJACK CUPS

200g raw butter

150g raw cane sugar

15g ground cinnamon

¾ teaspoon sea salt

½ teaspoon grated nutmeg

½ teaspoon ground ginger

250g oatmeal

40ml raw almond milk

Eccie and I have found ourselves eating the whole tray at once! The sweetness of the base is balanced out by the refreshing ice cream. These are perfect for a dinner party.

For the ice cream, put the bananas in a blender and blend until very smooth. Gradually add the almond milk, three-quarters of the honey and the xantham gum. Add a squeeze of lemon juice, stop the machine and taste the mixture. You may need to add a little more honey to get it sweet enough because, when frozen the sweetness will be a lot less apparent, so you want the mixture to be very slightly sweeter than you would like.

If you're using an ice-cream maker, switch it on and start it chilling. Pour in the almond mixture and set the timer for 50 minutes. If you're not using an ice-cream maker, place in a freezerproof container and put straight in the freezer for 1½ hours. When the ice cream is almost frozen, either in the machine, when the paddle begins to strain, or in the container in the freezer when it's fairly hard, remove and blend for 30 seconds. Return to the ice-cream maker or container in the freezer and continue to chill.

Meanwhile make the flapjack cups. Melt the butter at 35°C until just liquid, stir in the sugar and spices, remove from the heat and continue stirring. Once the sugar and spices are mixed in, add the oatmeal and coat them fully in the butter. Stir in the almond milk. Press the oat mixture onto the sides and bases of a 6–hole greased and lined muffin tin to form small cups. Freeze for 2 hours.

Scoop small balls of ice cream into the cups and freeze for 20 minutes. Use a spoon to release the cups from the muffin tin and serve.

AVOCADO AND CHOCOLATE MOUSSE TART

SERVES
8

4 ripe avocados, stoned and peeled

6 tablespoons raw cacao powder

about 5 tablespoons raw honey (depending on the sweetness of the avocado)

pinch of sea salt

squeeze of lemon

FOR THE BASE

1 tablespoon cold-pressed rapeseed oil

300g raw pecans

150g dates, stoned

This dessert really does not taste anything like avocado. It does taste a lot like very dark chocolate. One thing to remember is that because it sets like a mousse as it chills, once you've poured it onto the base, try not to disturb the mixture again; it ruins the set. Using the right avocados for this dish is also essential. Try to find South American avocados; those from Brazil are particularly good. They are twice the size of regular avocados (if you are using them, make sure that you use half as many) and are very sweet and so good in desserts and drinks, but not great in salads and dips.

Grease a 23cm tart tin with rapeseed oil, cut a thin strip of baking parchment the height of the tin and line the sides.

First make the base. Process the pecans and dates until they resemble fine breadcrumbs – the mixture will be sticky from the dates. Press the base mixture into the bottom of the tin so it's compact.

For the filling, blend the avocado, cacao powder, honey, salt and lemon juice together until very smooth. Check for taste at this point – it may need more honey. If so, add and blend for another 10 seconds, transfer into the tin and smooth down gently onto the base, working the mixture from the centre out, so you avoid pulling the parchment from the sides of the tin.

Freeze for 20–30 minutes, until the mixture has set. Remove from the tin and pull off the parchment.

RAW BANOFFEE PIE

SERVES
4

4 ripe bananas

500ml raw cream

25g flaked raw almonds

1 tablespoon raw cacao
powder

FOR THE BASE

25g raw butter

40ml raw almond milk

100g raw pecans

150g oatmeal

25g raw cane sugar

FOR THE SAUCE

100g raw butter

¼ teaspoon salt

8 tablespoons raw cane
sugar

½ teaspoon nutmeg

½ teaspoon ground ginger

3 teaspoons cinnamon

40ml raw almond milk

This is a dessert with a capital D. It's an all-singing,
all-dancing party piece that definitely doesn't want to
go home at midnight. We've used a lot of raw dairy
products here, which taste amazing and so much better
than their pasteurised equivalents.

Grease and line a 20cm tart tin.

For the base, melt the butter at 35°C. Combine the butter
with the milk. Blitz the pecans and oatmeal in a food
processor for 10 seconds then combine in a bowl with the
butter, milk and sugar. Press the mixture into the base and
sides of the tart tin. Freeze for 2 hours.

For the filling, thinly slice the bananas. Whip the cream until
it forms very soft peaks.

Combine the ingredients for the sauce and heat to 35°C so the
butter melts. Give everything a good mix then begin layering
the dessert.

Remove the tin from the freezer. First drizzle a couple of
tablespoons of sauce onto the base. Add a layer of banana
slices, add a layer of whipped raw cream, then add another
layer of banana slices and the flaked almonds. Drizzle over
the rest of the sauce. Dust with cacao.

ORANGE CHEESECAKE

SERVES
8

FOR THE BASE

200g raw butter

240g raw cane sugar

¾ teaspoon salt

1 teaspoon ground ginger

50g ground pistachios

70ml raw almond milk

400g oatmeal

FOR THE FILLING

175g raw cane sugar

2 free-range eggs, separated

250g soft mild goat's cheese
   (unpasteurised)

250g goat's curd
   (unpasteurised)

zest of 3 unwaxed oranges
   and 3 tablespoons
   orange juice

seeds scraped from
   1 vanilla pod

¾ teaspoon xanthum gum

seeds from 1 pomegranate

a handful of orange
   blossoms, optional

Not everyone would like the idea of goat's cheese in a cake, but the combination of orange and goat's cheese just works. We have added a small amount of xantham gum to help the cake set. If you can't get hold of this ingredient you can freeze the cheesecake instead which tastes just as good and is perfect for a warm summer's day. You can drizzle a little pomegranate molasses over the top, but note it's not strictly raw.

Grease and line a 23cm tart tin.

For the base, melt the butter at 35°C. Stir in the sugar, salt, ginger and ground pistachios, take off the heat and continue stirring. Add the almond milk. Once the sugar and spices are mixed in, add the oatmeal and stir to coat them fully in the buttery mixture. Press into the base and sides of the prepared tin. Freeze for 2 hours.

Now get on with the filling. In a freestanding mixer, whip the sugar with the egg yolks for 8–10 minutes at high speed until the mixture becomes thick and pale and resembles whipped cream. If you don't have a mixer you can whip the mixture over a bowl of steaming water.

In a separate clean bowl, whip the egg whites until very stiff and set aside. Beat the cheese, and curd, orange zest, juice and vanilla seeds into the egg yolks. Beat in a third of the egg white roughly to lighten the mix, then gently fold in the rest. Add the xantham gum to help the cheesecake set and mix well. Pour the mixture into the tart shell and leave in the fridge for 1 hour. Sprinkle with pomegranate seeds and, if using, orange blossom.

BEETROOT, BLACKBERRY & APPLE JUICE

This juice is a beautiful bright red, blend it like a smoothie or if you have a juicer pass it through that.

1 beetroot, scrubbed clean and cut into quarters (you can leave the skin on)

1 apple, pips and stalk removed

½ teaspoon peeled and grated ginger

3 parsley leaves

3 mint leaves

3 basil leaves

5 blackberries

70ml ice cold water

Using a high speed blender, blend all these ingredients together or pass all the ingredients through a juicer.

CARROT, GINGER & CITRUS JUICE

If you don't have a juicer, use a grater for the carrot and ginger and squeeze them using your hands to extract the juice.

1 orange

1 grapefruit

1 lime

2 carrots, peeled

2.5cm piece of peeled ginger

Juice the citrus fruits. Grate the carrot and ginger and squeeze out the juice, or blend and sieve.

MANGO LASSI

SERVES 1

We first tried mango lassi in Mumbai, where lassi is drunk everywhere. As soon as we got back, we started making it for breakfast every weekend. Freeze the whole tin of mango pulp (otherwise it will go off) and use it when needed.

425g tinned mango pulp

2 fresh mangoes, peeled and stoned

200ml raw almond milk or raw kefir

juice of ½ lemon

juice of 1 lime

½ long red chilli

2 mint leaves

3 basil leaves

60ml water (optional)

Freeze the mango pulp either in a freezerproof container or in an ice-cube tray.

Cut the fresh mangoes into slices and freeze.

Pour the almond milk or kefir into a blender with the citrus juice. Add ¼ tin of mango pulp, the mango slices, chilli and herbs.

Blend for 40–60 seconds until very smooth, adding water if the mixture is too thick and continue to blend.

STRAWBERRY-BASIL LEMONADE

MAKES 1 LITRE

The combination of aromatic basil, fresh strawberry and sour lemon is so refreshing.

juice of 6 lemons

5 tablespoons raw honey

500ml water

a small handful of basil leaves, torn

4 strawberries, sliced

ice, to serve

Pour the lemon juice into a 1-litre jug, stir in the honey and top up with water.

Add the basil leaves and strawberry slices.

Scoop ice into four tall glasses and top up with the lemonade.

GREEN SMOOTHIE

SERVES 2

Ok, so there's no kale, but this refreshing smoothie keeps all the fibre by blending all the fruits and veg rather than juicing.

1 apple

1 cucumber

a handful of mint leaves

a handful of basil leaves

juice of 2 limes

1 teaspoon grated, fresh ginger

Blend all the ingredients in a high speed blender for 30 seconds and sieve.

BASICS

PULP CAKES

MAKES 12 PULP CAKES

This is a savoury pulp cake that can be used as a substitute for bread, oatcakes or any base.

2 carrots

6 beetroots

6 tablespoons flax seeds

9 tablespoons raw almond flour or ground almonds

3 teaspoons nutritional yeast

. . . .

You can either use the pulp remains from beetroot and carrot juice that you have left in your blender or, using a cheese grater, grate the carrots and beetroot. Put all the ingredients in a blender and blend for 1 minute.

Make 12 thin circular pulp cakes and place on baking parchment or a tray ready for the dehydrator. Try to make sure the cakes have the same thickness throughout. Set the dehydrator at 37°C and leave the cakes in for 7–8 hours or bake them in the oven at its lowest setting for 15 hours. (It will take half the time in a dehydrator than it will in the oven because of better ventilation. If using an oven, place the pulp cakes on a rack above the tray to allow better ventilation.) You will need to flip the cakes halfway through the process so you get an even result.

Store in an airtight container in the fridge for up to a week.

SPICY TACOS

MAKES 8

These are perfect for breakfast with avocados (see page 23) or with Beef Tartare (see page 118) and Cashew Cream (see page 34). They are quite spicy so play around with the amounts of chilli powder and cayenne to your liking.

2 really fresh corn on the cob

juice of 2 lemons

2 red peppers, deseeded

4 tablespoons nutritional yeast

1 teaspoon cayenne pepper

1 teaspoon chilli powder

1 teaspoon dried oregano

4 tablespoons flax seeds

. . . .

Stand the corn cob upright on a board and cut down to slice off the kernels.

Put all the ingredients (except the flax seeds) in a blender and blend for 1 minute. Add the flax seeds in at the end and blend for another 5 seconds until the mixture is soft.

Flatten into 8 circular shapes on a sheet of baking parchment and put in a dehydrator at 37°C for 6 hours or in the oven on the lowest setting overnight.

They should be solid when they come out of the oven and are ready to eat.

Store in an airtight container in the fridge for up to a week.

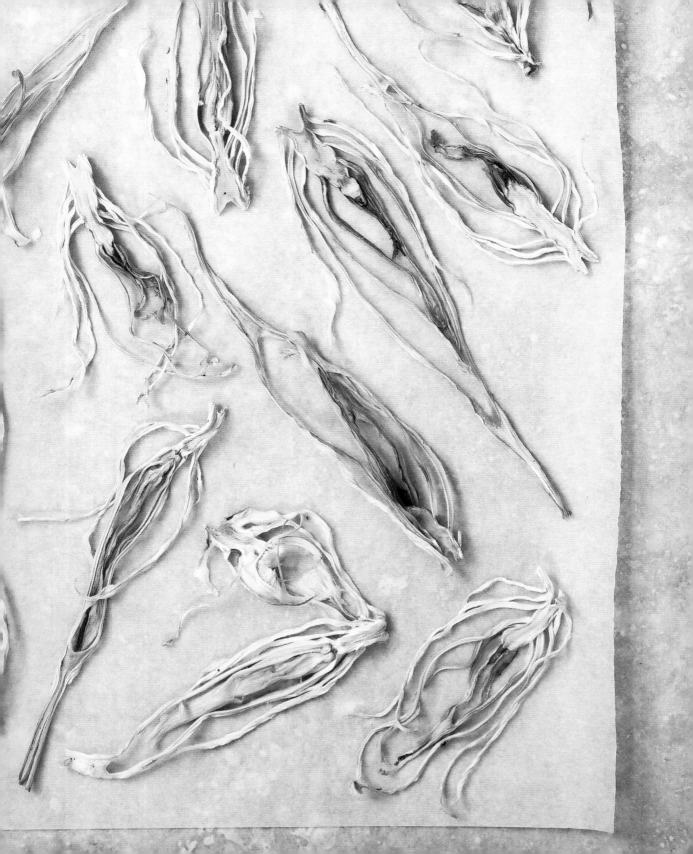

OVEN-DRIED FENNEL

When fennel is in season, oven-dry or dehydrate the bulbs with a little salt, garlic, lemon and olive oil.

2 fennel bulbs
1 teaspoon sea salt
1 garlic clove, crushed
1 teaspoon lemon juice
1 tablespoon cold-pressed extra virgin olive oil

Cut off the base of the fennel and remove the outermost layer of leaf.

Cut the fennel lengthways into 1cm thick slices, so that you can see all the interlocking layers of fennel, stalks and all. You can use a knife or a mandoline.

Put the oven on its lowest setting, or use a dehydrator if you have one. Spread the fennel out on baking parchment on a baking tray in a single layer and cover with the seasonings. Leave in the oven at its lowest setting or in a dehydrator at 37°C for around 6–8 hours. Store in an airtight container for up to four days.

DRIED CHERRY TOMATOES

Make a big batch of these and toss them into salads ot pasta dishes.

3kg cherry tomatoes, halved
1 teaspoon sea salt
1 teaspoon freshly ground black pepper

Arrange the tomatoes in a single layer on a tray, sprinkle with the salt and pepper and slip into the oven at its lowest setting overnight or the dehydrator at 37°C for 6–7 hours. The tomatoes should look soft and sticky at the end of the process. Store in an airtight container for up to four days.

SALTED CUCUMBER

Salting the cucumbers draws out a little of the water and makes them nice and crunchy. Partnered with sweet white miso this is a delicious snack and the fermented miso is full of good bacteria.

2 cucumbers

1 tablespoon salt

1 tablespoon sesame seeds

FOR THE DRESSING

4 tablespoons shiro miso (the lightest kind)

3 tablespoons raw acacia honey

1 tablespoon rice wine vinegar

2 teaspoons mirin (sweet rice wine)

Halve the cucumbers lengthways and scoop the seeds out with a small spoon, then slice diagonally. Mix the salt and 400ml iced water together in a bowl, add the cucumbers and leave for 20 minutes, then drain.

Mix the dressing ingredients together in a small bowl, pour the dressing over the cucumber slices and top with seeds.

CAULIFLOWER RICE

This is probably a lot easier than cooking rice is ever going to be. The people who invented the rice cooker told us all they had solved our problems of burnt pans and soggy goo. They lied! Our solution is to blitz cauliflower and stick it to the rice cooker man! Essentially all you need to do is put a cauliflower in a food processor. This then forms the base for a number of different recipes. Cauliflower has the pungent scent and flavour of raw brassicas just like sprouts, broccoli, and turnips, so we like to pair it with acids and fats to counterbalance those elements.

1 head of cauliflower

Remove the outer leaves of the cauliflower. Compost the big tough ones, and oven-dry the small ones with some salt and oil to snack on later.

Break the cauliflower head into even florets and cut the stalk into smallish chunks roughly the same size. This is so that when you blend it, you get an even texture. If the cauliflower is very small, you can put all the pieces in to blend at once, but otherwise, work in small batches to ensure an even texture. Make sure the food processor is never more than three-quarters full. Pulse for around 30 seconds, until the cauliflower resembles rice grains.

QUICK-CURED LEMONS

These lemon segments are cured in salt and oil and are great in salads or with fish or meat. The salt and oil combat the sourness of the lemon.

3 lemons
1 teapoon salt
150ml cold-pressed extra virgin olive oil

Using a small knife, cut the ends off the lemons down to the top of the flesh, stand the lemons up on a chopping board, then cut away the skin and the white pith so you are left with three peeled lemons.

Run the knife between each segment, with the blade facing outwards, so as to remove all the internal membranes separating the segments.

Squeeze the remaining juice from the hollowed out peel and membranes into a sterilised jar.

Pour in the salt and oil, give it a stir and pack in the lemon segments. Store in the fridge for up to one week.

5

DRESSINGS

GREEN MAN DRESSING

Bright green and full of herbs and vegetable, this is great on any salad.

1 garlic clove
1 small chilli
½ ripe avocado, stoned and peeled
juice of 2–3 lemons
a handful of coriander
a small handful of mint (stalks discarded)
a handful of flat-leaf parsley
a small handful of basil
1 spring onion
6 tablespoons cold-pressed extra
   virgin olive oil
1½ tablespoons tahini
sea salt and freshly ground black pepper

Put the garlic, chilli, avocado and lemon juice in a blender and blend roughly.

Chop the herbs and spring onion, add to the avocado mixture and blend for 20 seconds. Add the oil and tahini and blend for another 20 seconds, until very smooth and thick. Season with salt and pepper.

SESAME DRESSING

This works well with a spinach salad.

3 tablespoons tahini
½ teaspoon homemade mayo or Aioli
   (see page 157)
1 teaspoon raw cane sugar
1 teaspoon mirin (sweet rice wine)
2 tablespoons soy sauce or tamari
2 tablespoons sesame oil
2 tablespoons rice vinegar

Whisk all the ingredients vigorously in a bowl until very smooth.

SIMPLE LEMON DRESSING

This works well with a rocket salad.

juice of 1 lemon
1 tablespoon Dijon mustard
4 tablespoons cold-pressed extra
   virgin olive oil
1 teaspoon raw honey
½ garlic clove, grated (optional)

Mix all the ingredients together and serve with the salad of your choice.

AIOLI

MAKES 480 ML

This aioli is the base for many recipes. It's incredibly versitile and when made with wonderful cold-pressed oils and a fresh organic egg, there's no reason to feel like it's an unhealthy choice.

1 free-range egg yolk

1 teaspoon sea salt

2 tablespoons Dijon mustard

180ml cold-pressed extra virgin olive oil

180ml cold-pressed rapeseed oil

juice of 2–3 lemons

2 garlic cloves, crushed

In a large heavy mixing bowl, mix the egg yolk with the salt and the mustard.

Pour the oils into a jug or squeeze bottle so you can control how much you pour in at a time. Drizzle in the oil drop by drop and slowly whisk in each drop until it has disappeared before adding the next drop.

After a quarter of the oil has been added, whisk in a quarter of the lemon juice. Begin adding the oil again, pouring in a thin constant stream while you whisk the egg. The aioli will gradually thicken. As it gets thick, pour in the rest of the lemon juice gradually – the mixture will thin and turn paler – then continue adding the remainder of the oil until it is all incorporated. Stir in the crushed garlic.

Store in the fridge for up to a day.

YOGHURT & TAHINI DRESSING

Though some yogurt is heated to pasteurise it, this often happens before it's fermented and it's during this fermentation period that the main enzyme activity begins to change the nature of the milk into something magical. This dressing is rich, and works well with vegetables and strong spices or hot food.

3 tablespoons natural live yogurt

5 tablespoons cold-pressed extra virgin olive oil

2 tablespoons tahini

½ teaspoon sea salt

juice of 2 lemons

Mix all the ingredients in a bowl until the tahini and yogurt look very smooth (it sometimes goes through a midway curdled-looking phase). Add a little water at a time, so it becomes silky smooth.

INDEX

THANK-YOU

to our agent Claudia Young,

our photographer and friend Issy Croker,

food stylist Annie Nichols,

props sytlist Iris Bromet,

designer Anita Mangan

and to our publisher Kyle Cathie.